REMARKABLE WOMEN *of* OAKLAND COUNTY, MICHIGAN

CHRISTINE BLACKWELL

THE History PRESS

Published by The History Press
An imprint of Arcadia Publishing
Charleston, SC
www.historypress.com

First published 2025

Manufactured in the United States

ISBN 9781467158220

Library of Congress Control Number: 2025940389

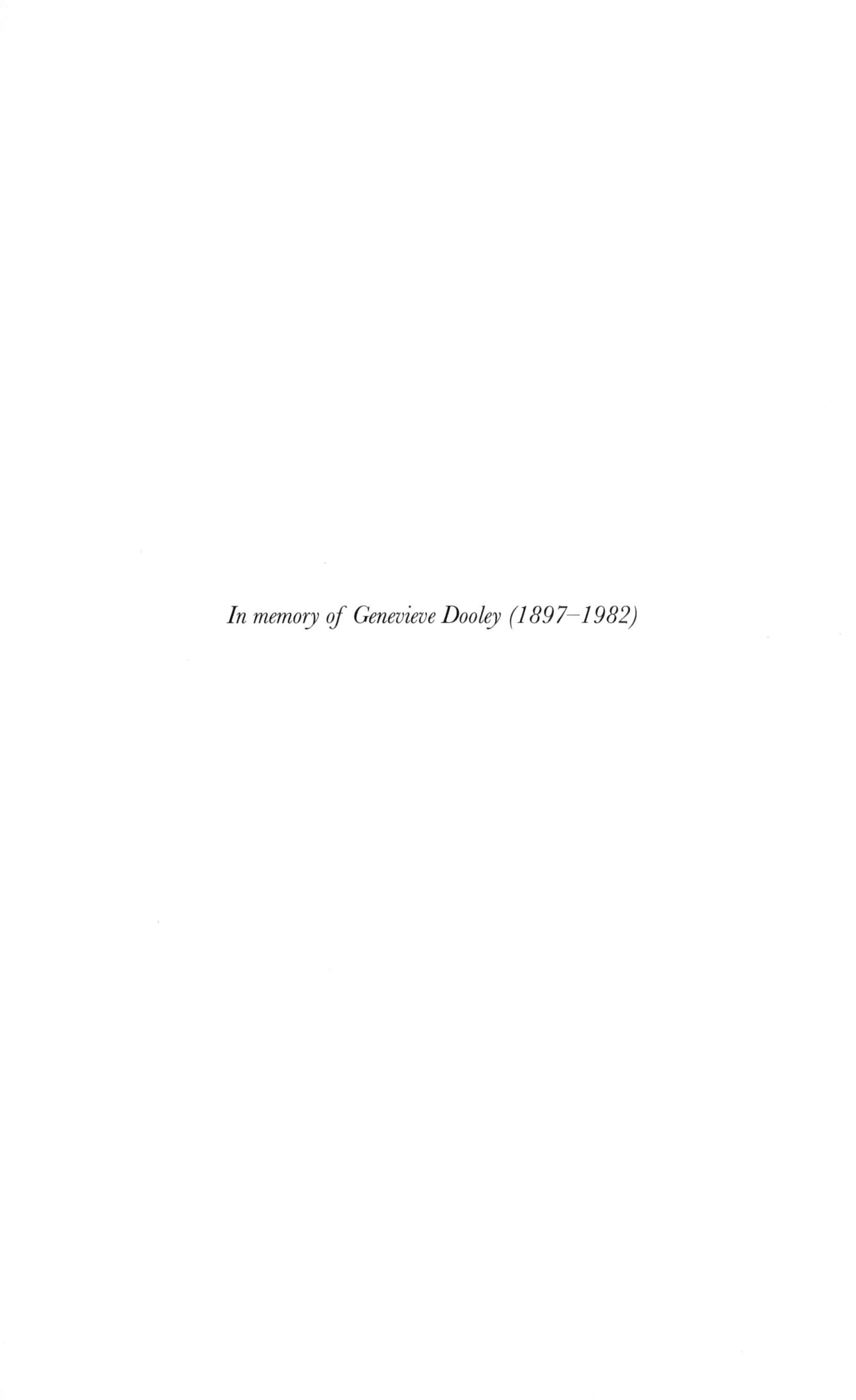

In memory of Genevieve Dooley (1897–1982)

CONTENTS

ACKNOWLEDGEMENTS

A big thank-you goes to my editor, John Rodrigue, for his advice, editing and patience and for giving me the opportunity to write about this topic. Thanks also to Zoe Ames, copyeditor extraordinaire on this book. I also express my gratitude to Robin Roberts, president of the Lathrup Village Historical Society, for her review of the history of Louise Lathrup Kelley. Ditto to Marcia Ruff, historian at the Roeper School, as well as to the marketing staff at Meadow Brook Hall for their review of the text about Matilda Dodge Wilson. Thank you also to Samantha Lawrence at the Rochester Hills Museum at Van Hoosen Farm for her review of selected sections. Denny Dinan-Panico also has my appreciation for her wonderful advice and suggestions. Barbara Frye, secretary of the Oakland County Pioneer & Historical Society, graciously helped me locate hard-to-find photos and contributed a feature to the book. I would be remiss if I didn't also say thank you to my fabulous stylist friends Julie Spasoski, Minoo and Sandy Ortman, as well as to my friend from childhood Debbie Stevens for listening to me talk about this project for nearly a year (and who made me laugh when I most needed to do so). When I sometimes grew tired from working long hours on this project, I talked with Andreise Souza, a former student of mine who showed me what tenacity can achieve. She arrived in the United States a few years ago from Brazil determined to become a physician and studied English with me. She stands tall now as Andreise Souza, MD, physician with Corewell Health. Kathleen Tillson of NEXT in Birmingham was extremely patient and gracious whenever I needed help using the center's computers or printers. Last but not least, I would like to thank four gentlemen of Oakland County who have graciously helped me whenever I requested it: historians John Marshall and Bruce Annett; Jason from Bloomfield Deli, for his helpful comments; and my brother, Norm Blackwell, who shared his recollections.

I am not afraid.
I was born to do this.
—Joan of Arc

INTRODUCTION

There must be something in the water," I said to myself as I began researching the number of remarkable women who were born, lived or worked in Oakland County. With more than 1,400 freshwater lakes and streams and a population of more than 1.2 million, Oakland County has plenty of water and remarkable women to "write home about"—so many, in fact, that I had a hard time narrowing down my list of women to include in this book. Many women here have made or are continuing to make valuable contributions to our local, state and national history, yet there has been no previously published book that gathers together their life stories. I realized immediately that I could easily write at least three volumes of local women's biographies and still not have scratched much below the surface.

Thankfully, my publisher, The History Press, provided me with the constraints I needed: a maximum number of words and a deadline. By the end of my writing journey, I found that I was able to include the biographies of thirty-nine women. Of this total, I was surprised to learn, more than two-thirds were or are married and have children. How did they manage to balance work and family? A few, such as Dr. Petra Huck, provide insights or suggestions.

In this volume, you will read about women from the 1800s to the present. Their stories range from a few hundred words to two thousand words. The earliest histories include those of women such as Hazel Donlon, who was born in 1897 and became an executive for the Burton Abstract Company when there were few other such women executives. At the other end of the spectrum—and living very much in the present while looking to the future—is Mary Barra, CEO of General Motors.

One goal I had in writing this book, in addition to recording women's histories before their stories were lost to time, was to inspire the next generation of women who are coming of age. If you ask many such young women who their heroes are, beyond their immediate family members, most cannot name any. As our world grows increasingly complex, these women can use all the inspiration they can get. This book presents both historical and modern-day role models and their life stories. It includes words of wisdom from successful women about ways younger women can begin achieving productive, worthwhile lives of their own.

If you are a promising young builder or dream of becoming an architect, you might benefit from reading about Louise Lathrup Kelley and how she developed an entire city of homes called Lathrup Village. If your goal is a career in law, read about Hilda Gage, who overcame a disability to become a top judge. Want to pilot a plane or write a novel? Then read about author Anne Morrow Lindbergh, who achieved both goals. She lived in Oakland County for only two years but soared literally and figuratively by flying with her husband, Charles, and writing her first novel here. If entertainment success is your goal, read about the paths that Aretha Franklin, Kristen Bell, Christine Lahti and others took to achieve success.

Perhaps the most compelling reason to read these histories, in addition to enjoying moments of nostalgia, is to better appreciate the hard work and sacrifices made by those who came before us. Oakland County is one of the wealthiest counties in the state and a great place to live. Was our county always like this, or was some planning and hard work involved? Who were some of the first women who moved here? What were their struggles, and how did they overcome them? What did they achieve and how? How did each one help her community?

This book is divided into twelve chapters with two or more short biographies per chapter. A special feature after every three chapters is a woman's history told in her own words. The first chapter presents the history of a pioneer woman who traveled here with her husband to make both a home and a living from the land. The final chapter shares three histories of women who, in different ways, have come full circle with that first biography. Each has worked as a farmer or environmentalist to make good use of our resources so that they will be available for future generations—not a bad way to use the past to create an even better future for Oakland County!

Chapter 1
PIONEERS AND REFORMERS

Hannah Ann Newman (Born 1812)

PONTIAC TOWNSHIP

In 1835, when newly married Hannah Ann Newman (née Fisher) was twenty-three, she and her husband, Justin, moved from New York to Pontiac Township in Oakland County.[1] As was typical at that time, they traveled to Michigan Territory by steamboat from Buffalo to Detroit via the Erie Canal. The Erie Canal was considered a wondrous feat of engineering that enabled westward transportation and thus the settlement by pioneers of new lands in the Northwest Territory.

However, the journey was not an easy one. Once the steamboat arrived, Hannah and Justin—already tired from their water journey—were met by Mr. Axford, who transported them by wagon to their place of settlement. The lumber wagon on which they traveled was pulled by two teams of horses but was bereft of seats for Hannah and Justin, so they had to endure their journey accordingly for five days before reaching their destination. Without roads, this meant traveling "through the woods, over obstacles, and through streams" in varying weather before arriving at their twelve-by-fourteen-foot log cabin home.[2] The Newmans were more fortunate than many other pioneers as they had a constructed log cabin awaiting them. Other pioneers stayed in inns or taverns while they built their own cabins.

The Craig Log Cabin at Bowers School Farm is representative of the log cabins built during the early nineteenth century in Oakland County. *Author's collection.*

Justin Newman had purchased 160 acres in Pontiac Township. The land was noted as having a lot of timber, making it more valuable than if it had been cleared. Nonetheless, hard work would still be required to cut the timber and clear the land, as well as fortitude to deal with discomforts and dangers such as mosquitoes, wolves, bears and poisonous snakes, including the venomous Massasauga rattlesnake.[3] Additionally, in their future, diseases ranging from ague to influenza to smallpox would be common; the latter was known to wipe out whole families.

Nevertheless, Hannah and Justin survived these perils and lived in their cabin for three years before building a larger one. Then, in 1854, they built a more comfortable residence for themselves. Justin lived the life of a farmer until December 1882, when he passed away. By then, the couple had enjoyed nearly forty-eight years of marriage. Notably, due to his and Hannah's efforts, the Baptist Church of Oakland had been organized as well as supported by them.

Together, Hannah and Justin had eight children, who then produced sixteen grandchildren and five great-grandchildren, all during Hannah's lifetime. The family was noted as being "closely bound" and "affectionate." As for Hannah, she claimed she was "personally acquainted with Chief Pontiac and many of his braves" and said she remembered when the chief died. During the Civil War, she volunteered her time to secure provisions for the soldiers who were fighting, and according to written accounts, she was highly esteemed in Oakland County. However, the date of her own death was not recorded.[4]

Hannah Ann Newman's published pioneer history in Edward C. Smith's *Biographical Record: Biographical Sketches of Leading Citizens of Oakland County, Michigan* is a bit longer than most. Most pioneer women became wives and mothers, and typically, only their names and those of their spouse(s), children and grandchildren, along with birth, marriage and death dates, are provided in published records. Nonetheless, pioneer women inherited all the duties associated with their marital status, while their husbands usually took care of the farm or other business duties and thus were more public-facing.

One famous local granddaughter of pioneers, Martha Baldwin of Birmingham (see her history beginning on page 81), wrote an article about Oakland County pioneer women titled "What Women Have Done for Oakland County," which was published in Thaddeus D. Seeley's *History of Oakland County*. In it, she describes some of the typical work done by pioneer women.

> *The part that women have taken in the building up of Oakland County can never be fully told....She walked beside the ox-teams that were drawing the household goods; she helped to build the log house; she planted the tiny seed whence came the orchards for which the county was soon to be famous.... She helped to build the schoolhouse and gathered the little ones within its walls....She tended the sick and went miles on errands of mercy. She carded the wool, spun the yarn, wove the cloth, bleached the flax, baked in the out-of-door oven, made the garden, and then mended and patched the garments of the sleeping children till morning hours. The floors must be scrubbed, for there were no carpets; the fruit must be dried, for there were no fruit cans; the candles must be dipped; the geese must be picked; the children must be helped with their lessons.*[5]

No record exists of the actual work that Hannah and Justin did. However, it is likely that Hannah completed more than a few of the tasks described by Martha Baldwin. This much is known: the land on which Hannah and Justin built their home became part of the state of Michigan on January 26, 1837.

Rachel Andresen (1907–1988)

SOUTH LYON

Following the devastation of World War II, Rachel Andresen saw the residual resentment and hatred of some people toward others in countries they had been at war with, and she came to believe that, moving forward, the world's young people were the sole hope for creating future peace in the world.[6] In 1947, after she flew over post–World War II ruins in Europe while on a visit with her husband, she said, "I wondered how it would ever be possible to rebuild what had been destroyed.[7] Even more importantly, what has been damaged within the people's lives and hearts. What could I ever do?"[8]

Rachel Andresen. *Courtesy of the South Lyon Historical Society.*

Rachel Andresen would do more than she might have ever imagined. She went on to found and direct Youth for Understanding (YFU), a successful exchange program for high school students that is still going strong. Its purpose is to promote intercultural understanding, mutual respect and social responsibility.[9] Today, the YFU network consists of member organizations in forty-five different countries.[10]

Over her lifetime, Rachel Andresen received many honors and awards. These included honorary degrees and citations from U.S. presidents, state governors, foreign government leaders and members of the United Nations. She was nominated for the Nobel Peace Prize.[11] In 1991, she was inducted into the Michigan Woman's Hall of Fame.[12]

Rachel Andresen was born Rachel Josephine Mills in Deerfield, Michigan, on April 8, 1907. Her parents were the Reverend Earl R. Mills, a Methodist minister, and his wife, Josephine Mills.[13] As a teenager, she attended and graduated from Adrian High School. Afterward, she studied music at the Detroit Conservatory of Music, using her training to give piano lessons.[14] In 1927, she married Henry C. Rose, an engineering student at the University of Michigan, with whom she had three children. Once Henry graduated and was beginning to establish himself as an engineer, he became ill with encephalitis during the epidemic of 1934 and died.[15] Widowed at age twenty-eight in the midst of the Great Depression, Rachel was left to raise her children on her own. She found that she had few paying customers for piano lessons during that period, so she decided to return to school for more education as a way to help her find employment.[16]

In 1937, Rachel graduated from Wayne State University with a BS degree in education. Afterward, she began working for the YWCA, and in 1942, she purchased a farmhouse on eighty-two acres in South Lyon, which she used as both a hostel for travelers and a summer camp. She continued her studies, and in 1943, she earned a master's degree in social work from the University of Michigan.

During the remainder of the 1940s, she worked in various capacities, including as a group counselor, a camp director of the summer camp program she had set up on her own farm as a youth retreat and a race relations and social action director for the Michigan Council of Churches. In 1947, when she was forty, she married Arvid Andreson, a Danish-born landscape architect who had once stayed at her hostel.[17]

By 1951, she was working as the executive director of the Ann Arbor-Washtenaw Council of Churches when local Rotary clubs contacted her and presented her with the challenge of finding homes for seventy-five German teenagers, a challenge she accepted. These young people had been selected by the U.S. State Department to live with American families and attend high schools here "in an effort to counteract the bitterness and disillusionment of youth in post–World War II Germany."[18]

At first, Rachel was apprehensive about how the program might work. But then the first teenagers from Germany arrived to live with American host families, and the program began to show success almost immediately. At the end of their stay in the United States, the German exchange students gathered as a group to say farewell and were met by hundreds of local people, including their host families, teachers and fellow students, who turned out to wish them well. Rachel realized then that it is difficult for people to hate each other or even a country once they get to know each other and gain understanding at the family or community level. This concept formed the basic idea behind YFU.[19]

In 1952, Rachel received a formal request from the Rotarians and the State Department to supervise the entire program. The Michigan Council of Churches later adopted this program, which was expanded to include students from other countries, as well as to send American students overseas to study and live with host families, effectively creating a robust international student exchange program.

By 1955, the first American teenagers were traveling to Scandinavian countries during their summer break and living with families there for ten weeks. The program soon expanded to numerous other countries in Western and Central Europe. The exchange program was so successful that in 1958, Rachel received the Knights Cross of the Order of Merit from President Heuss of the Federal Republic of West Germany. Six years later, she was presented with the Order of Merit of the Lion of Finland by President Kekkonen.

The expansion continued as former exchange students and host families spread the word and promoted the program. In 1958, the first exchange students from Japan arrived in the United States. The Pacific program grew to include exchange students from Australia, South Korea, the Philippines, Vietnam, Thailand and China. Later that year, YFU was established in Mexico. It expanded to South American countries in 1959, and the Ministry of Education of Brazil presented Rachel with the Grand Cross of the Order of the Albatross and the Gold Medal of Marechal Rondon.[20] By 1972, the program had become so successful that Rachel Andresen was honored by President Richard Nixon and more than sixty members of Congress at a congressional reception and black tie dinner. In 1973, she was nominated for the Nobel Peace Prize.[21]

Rachel Andresen served as the executive director of the YFU program until 1973, when she retired. However, that milestone by no means meant she had retired from life. She was appointed and given the lifetime title of Honorary International President of the Youth for Understanding Teenage Exchange Program. That same year, she was appointed by Governor Milliken to the Commission for Volunteers in Michigan, and she went on to win the Republican nomination for supervisor of Green Oak Township.

On November 3, 1988, Rachel Andresen, age eighty-one, died in her hometown of South Lyon, Michigan.[22] Youth for Understanding continues today with headquarters in Saginaw, Michigan, and Washington, D.C.

Chapter 2
BUSINESS LEADERS

Hazel A. Donlon (Born 1897)

ROYAL OAK

Hazel A. Donlon was an executive in Oakland County when there were few other women in such positions. In 1918, she was named secretary and treasurer for the Fred Burton Abstract Company in the Tribune Building in Royal Oak, where she "exercised full management" of the company.[23] The Burton Abstract and Title Company is still operating today.

Hazel was born on October 3, 1897, in Detroit to Anna and John Donlon. Her parents sent her to a parochial school in Detroit, and they later moved with Hazel to Florida after her father retired from the wholesale candy business. Hazel finished high school in Florida but afterward returned with her parents to Detroit to live.

She continued her education by attending the Central Business College in Detroit. During 1921–22, when she was already working, she attended the University of Detroit. She had been hired initially as a messenger for Fred Burton at the Burton Abstract Company. However, due to her industriousness and ability, "which carried her through every department of the business, [she] was elevated to the general management in 1918."[24]

In 1920, the rapidly growing company expanded its operations to Royal Oak, initially operating with only two employees but soon employing twelve

Hazel Donlon *(front, left). Courtesy of the Burton Historical Collection, Detroit Public Library.*

people. In addition to Hazel Donlon serving as secretary and treasurer, Fred Burton continued as president and Clarence Burton as vice president. Hazel also became active in associated business and social organizations. She was a member of the Chamber of Commerce, the Welfare Committee and the Business and Professional Women's Clubs.

Of note, Hazel's boss, Clarence Burton, went on to establish the Burton Historical Collection, and his son, Frank Burton, donated the entire collection to the Detroit Public Library, including the above photo of Hazel when she first began working for the company.

LOUISE LATHRUP KELLEY (1893–1963)

LATHRUP VILLAGE

The little homes that hold
Such power to soothe and bless;
They're packed with joys untold—
Gateways to Happiness!

The above stanza from "Gateways to Happiness," a poem by Anne Campbell, was included in the 144-page book *Gateways to Happiness*. The book was written and copyrighted in 1924 by land developer Louise Lathrup and given as a gift to lot buyers in her new one-thousand-acre townsite development called Southfield Village.[25] In her book, Louise extolled the pleasures that her customers would enjoy when they built their homes in her development. That development was later called Lathrup Townsite, and by 1953, it had been incorporated as the City of Lathrup Village.

Louise Lathrup was one of only a few female land developers in the United States at the time. According to a 2022 report from the U.S. Bureau of Labor Statistics, women still make up only 10.9 percent of the construction workforce, including developers.[26] Nonetheless, by age thirty-one, Louise was already selling lots in her second housing development in the Detroit area. Her start in land development came to her via unusual family circumstances.

Born on April 20, 1893, as Hannah Lathrup, Louise, as she came to be called, was the first of six children born to Annie Mallender and John Wesley Lathrup in Greenfield Township, now part of Dearborn, Michigan. After high school, Louise attended business college. She then worked, for one year, as a clerk for the Ford Motor Company in Highland Park. In 1918, her parents divorced, and Louise's mother, Annie, received land in Detroit rather than money as alimony. Not knowing what to do with the land, Annie turned over the development and management of her property to her daughter.[27]

Louise took her new project seriously. She created design standards for the former farm property on Lawrence and Collingwood Avenues between Dexter Boulevard and Linwood Avenue. She had come to appreciate the Tudor and cottage styles of architecture from her paternal grandmother, Miami Woodworth Lathrup, who was of English descent, but she also admired the bungalow and Spanish Mission styles she had seen on a visit to California.[28] Different architectural styles would be allowed in her

Louise Lathrup Kelley hands the keys to open the new post office in the City of Lathrup Village to Postmaster Veld E. Blue, April 1956. © *Detroit Free Press/USA TODAY NETWORK.*

development, but she required that she preapprove all the designs and that the homes be of all brick construction. The lots sold quickly. Louise later referred to the attractiveness of the finished homes and the success of that development as she began to develop her next project.

From 1917 to 1923, Annie and Louise bought land in Oakland County's Southfield Township. Both mother and daughter could already see, during their weekly trips to Birmingham to visit family members, that the population was growing northward. New multilane roads were being built, which meant access for more cars and people. And more people meant the need for more homes. The land the Lathrups had purchased was still mostly farmland, but it was strategically located, so their chances of successfully developing it and building a residential community appeared excellent. By the mid-1920s, Louise had acquired one thousand acres of the land that would eventually become the City of Lathrup Village. Louise, with her mother's approval, accepted total responsibility for the property's development, referring to it as her "thousand-acre garden city."[29]

By coincidence, the Lathrup surname in Old English means "a group of country homes or a hamlet."[30] Perhaps Louise's paternal grandmother, Miami, provided this information to Louise at the same time she shared her fondness for Tudor architecture with her. Nonetheless, the meaning of Louise's surname would be realized one day as she developed her new community in a country setting.

During 1919, Louise married John Brophy, about whom little is known except that the marriage did not last; by 1924, the couple had divorced. In 1924, Louise met Charles Darrell Kelley, a real estate editor for *The Detroit News*, who shared Louise's interests in land development and home building. They soon became a couple, and Charles advised Louise on her selection of architects for her new community of homes.

The year 1924 was fortuitous for Louise in another way. She had published and was already distributing her book *Gateways to Happiness* to prospective lot buyers in her new Southfield Village development. Within the year, the book went into a second printing. Her goal of building a high-quality planned community that included California bungalow–style homes was coming true. Once again, she set strict standards for the houses' designs and construction and preapproved all building plans.

The homes included amenities and features that many middle-class homeowners had not experienced before. Planned zoning restrictions mandated single-family residences only, attached garages, masonry (brick, stone or cement stucco) construction, basements with incinerators, extra-large lots with forty-foot setbacks, sidewalks, landscaping with trees and winding paved roads. In the early years, shuttle service to the nearest shopping center and transportation hubs into Detroit was also offered.

Louise also suggested that lot purchasers use architects she (and Charles) recommended to design and build their homes—prominent architects such as J. Ivan Dise, John B. Jewell, J.H.G. Steffens and F. Orla Varney. Louise provided a host of planning services that included a choice of 125 house plans complete with elevations, specifications and working drawings.

In 1925, the first bungalow-style home was built—ironically, on Bungalow Street. As of March 20, 1925, the least expensive home, called Annie's Little House, could be financed and built for $10,302. The most expensive model, called the Cadillac, could be built for $31,200. That same year, Louise began building a 10,600-square-foot home for herself on six and a half acres of the Southfield Township land. She named it House-in-the-Woods and began living there two years later.[31] The house, which was designed by architect J. Ivan Dise, had five fireplaces, three kitchens, seven bedrooms, five full baths, two half bathrooms and a three-car garage.[32]

The Annie Lathrup Elementary School and the Town Hall Sales Office were built in 1926 as focal points for the community along the "superhighway" of Southfield Road.[33] Although the attractive Tudor-style school building would close five decades later, by 1999, it was included in the Lathrup Village Local Historic District, and it remains on the National Register of Historic Places.

Only a few days before the stock market crash in 1929 and the beginning of the Great Depression, Louise married Charles D. Kelley. They lived and worked together in House-in-the-Woods, which became their combined home and sales office. On October 17, 1930, Louise gave birth to a daughter, whom they named Louise Lathrup Kelley.

Out of necessity, the family soon moved from House-in-the-Woods into the second floor of the Town Hall, which served as the couple's Southfield Road business headquarters. The Great Depression was taking a toll on

House-in-the-Woods. *Courtesy of the Burton Historical Collection, Detroit Public Library.*

home sales, and the Kelleys put House-in-the-Woods up for sale to save on expenses. However, the nation's financial situation dragged on for several more years, and in 1936, the Kelleys mortgaged their home because they continued to be unsuccessful in selling it.

As the Depression continued, Louise's debts mounted. Sales and construction had stopped, and she faced the additional difficulty of getting lot owners to pay on their land contracts. In 1936, the Kelleys took out a land contract on their house and several other properties they owned, but they became delinquent on their payments. By 1939, they had put House-in-the-Woods up for sale for a mere $75,000, but they still had no takers. Nonetheless, the Kelleys finally found a way to keep their home. By receiving an FHA mortgage, which they used to pay off their land contract, they were able to pay off their home by 1953.

The townsite development itself began to recover slowly in the late 1930s. Following World War II, sales picked up considerably, and Louise found that she was back in business developing her beloved garden village of homes.

House-in-the-Woods did get used in various capacities after the Kelleys moved out. The Lathrup Village Women's Club held meetings there. Then, from 1953 to 1962, it was used as Lathrup Village's first city hall. Later, the Kelleys' daughter, Louise, lived in the home.

Unfortunately, in 2009, House-in-the-Woods was struck by lightning and burned. The damage was quite severe, so the house was torn down. The land on which the house sat has since become woods, but it might become available for development, as buyers in the recent past have expressed an interest in purchasing and subdividing the property.

In 1953, the City of Lathrup Village became the first incorporated community in Southfield Township. The community's timing in seeking incorporation was fortuitous, because simultaneously, Southfield petitioners were pushing for all areas of Southfield Township, including Lathrup Village, to become the City of Southfield. However, Lathrup Village had filed its own petition for incorporation slightly earlier than Southfield and thus succeeded in becoming a separate city. In 1958, the City of Southfield incorporated; today, it completely surrounds the City of Lathrup Village.[34]

Louise stayed active with the city until her death on January 25, 1963, at age sixty-nine. Afterward, her remaining real estate holdings in the city were sold and developed by others. She is buried in Woodlawn Cemetery, as are Charles Kelley (1882–1966) and Annie Lathrup (1861–1954).

Today, the Lathrup Village Historic District includes about 1,200 primarily residential properties encompassing approximately one and a half square miles. Its population hovers just above four thousand. The housing styles include Colonial Revival, Spanish Colonial Revival, Tudor, English Cottage and ranch homes.[35]

The City of Lathrup Village remains a testament to the hard work and dedication of Louise Lathrup. It is a crowning achievement in the history of American city development. A representative from the Michigan State Historic Preservation Office said this about Louise and Lathrup Village: "As a woman acting as a developer starting in the 1920s, she was essentially alone; however, her dogged persistence and insistence on quality resulted in a unique community that was the summation of her career."[36]

Robin Roberts, president of the Lathrup Village Historical Society, perhaps said it best when describing Lathrup Village's namesake: "Louise was a fascinating woman. The company records survived the House-in-the-Woods fire; they show that she was involved in every decision. I think that she would be amazed at what the city has become."

Mary Barra

WATERFORD TOWNSHIP

Mary Barra is the first female chief executive officer (CEO) and chair of General Motors (GM), one of the largest and most powerful companies in the world. She is also the first female CEO of any of the Big Three auto companies. Her accolades since she became CEO have been numerous. In both 2024 and 2025, she was named No. 1 on *Fortune* magazine's Most Powerful Women in Business list. Twice before, she had made *Fortune*'s list of the Most Powerful Women in large corporations in the world. She has also appeared on the cover of *Time* magazine twice as one of the world's one hundred most influential people, and in 2023, she was inducted into the Automotive Hall of Fame.

These honors are the result of her leadership at GM, where she has worked for more than three decades. In the fall of 2024, the company reported its strongest financial position in more than seventeen years, with more than $10 billion in profits and the company's stock up by 35 percent.

Mary Barra believes that we are in the midst of a transportation revolution as new technologies are rapidly changing how people will interact with vehicles in the very near future. Changes in the political and

Mary Barra. *Courtesy of Wikimedia Commons.*

economic climates might require her to pivot as necessary to meet changing market demands.[37] Nonetheless, throughout 2024, Mary Barra remained committed to GM moving toward producing electric vehicles (EVs) by 2035 and being a leader in producing autonomous cars. She has used the phrase "zero zero zero" several times in interviews, explaining that she and GM are moving toward "zero crashes, zero emissions and zero congestion." Her vision for EVs includes the possibility of bi-directional charging, in which EVs become a source of energy for the grid, meaning that energy can be sold back to the grid. Achieving sustainability in the auto industry through fuel efficiency and other methods for future generations is also part of this overall vision.[38]

Her rise to the top of GM has come with her ability to navigate and overcome considerable business challenges over the years, one of which occurred almost immediately after she was appointed CEO in January 2014. That same year, she had to testify at a hearing before Congress regarding the GM safety recall of 2.6 million cars due to a serious faulty ignition switch problem, which resulted in deaths and serious accidents and, ultimately, a payout of millions of dollars. However, this situation also led Mary to develop strong new policies for GM, changing the corporate culture to be more transparent. Her "Speak Up for Safety" campaign requires all employees to report problems immediately so they can be solved as soon as possible. Other challenges that she has been able to successfully address since 2014 include the rapid manufacturing of ventilators needed during the COVID-19 pandemic, the 2023 autoworker strike and issues with battery production and the need for more semiconductors. Her leadership style includes advocating for open communication, employee empowerment and a commitment to both integrity and accountability.[39]

Mary Barra knows that she is a role model for many young people but particularly for women, and she takes that responsibility seriously. In recent interviews, she was asked, "What advice would you give to young women who hope to have successful careers in business?" Her advice included getting a good education and taking courses in STEM (science, technology, engineering and mathematics), even if, later in their careers, women choose to change fields. She has noted that many young women stop taking STEM courses as early as middle school, even when they do well in them. She strongly advocates for all young women learning to code and taking technical courses, especially by completing advanced placement courses, if possible, which can be helpful when applying to college.[40]

Most importantly, she has repeatedly emphasized that more women need to speak up. "Find your voice. Have a point of view, and, of course, work hard." She has noticed that many women hesitate to speak up, in business meetings in particular. "Perhaps they're thinking it [a good idea or a solution to a problem], and then someone else speaks up instead. You might not be right, but no one is right every time." What tip does she offer for how young women can overcome their fear of speaking up? "When you get that little uncomfortable feeling in your stomach, that's when you really need to go for it."[41]

So how did Mary Barra begin her own career? In 1961, Mary Teresa Makela was born in Royal Oak, the daughter of Ray and Eva Makela (née Pyykkonen), who were both of Finnish descent. Her father was a die maker for GM in Pontiac for nearly forty years, and her mother was a bookkeeper. Although neither of Mary's parents had earned a college degree, they believed that getting a good education was important and wanted to ensure that Mary and her brother, Paul, went to college. This was particularly true of Mary's mother, Eva, who insisted that both Mary and Paul attend, and they both did so successfully. Mary's brother became a physician.

Mary grew up in Waterford Township, attending public schools and graduating from Waterford Mott High School in 1980. She did exceptionally well throughout school, enjoying her math and science courses in particular, and her parents encouraged her to pursue those interests further. She also loved cars from an early age and remembers tinkering with them with her father in their garage. She also has memories of taking apart other pieces of equipment when they needed repair, such as her curling iron, which gave her an understanding of how the equipment worked. She graduated as one of ten students in her class who achieved a perfect 4.0 GPA. She was also voted the girl most likely to succeed. However, former classmates also remember Mary as being personable and able to talk to everybody in the school regardless of their interests or background.

With a strong work ethic encouraged and modeled by her parents, Mary worked part time while attending high school at a local grocery store in Pontiac called Felice's Quality Market. Like many of her classmates during that time, she also participated in typical after-school activities such as going with friends to Pontiac Mall (later called Summit Mall).

By her senior year of high school, Mary was already demonstrating strong managerial skills in her role as coeditor of her high school yearbook, Polaris. That job required her to work with a lot of different personalities while also ensuring that deadlines were met and standards were achieved. She shared this job with a classmate, who said that Mary was noticeably gifted at pulling the staff together and getting everyone to work as a team, for which she has since become renowned at GM.

Following graduation from Waterford Mott High School, she hoped to major in mathematics at Michigan State University (MSU). However, her parents had been able to save enough money for her to attend for only one year, so completing a four-year bachelor's degree at MSU seemed uncertain. Then, just before she was to leave to attend MSU, a friend told her about the cooperative program at General Motors Institute (GMI), now called Kettering University, where she could alternate studying and working for wages that would enable her to pay for college herself. Mary found this option attractive because she thought it was the most responsible course of action she could take, considering that her father was already retired and her mother was working part time.[42]

Once enrolled in the program at GMI, she began her training in industrial management. First, she was assigned to work at an assembly plant in Pontiac, where she experienced what it was like for assemblers to work in a factory environment. She also learned what it felt like to meet production goals from the manager's viewpoint, and she witnessed the tensions that sometimes developed between workers and managers. As her father had been a member of the United Auto Workers (UAW), she already knew about unions, but at the plant, she had what she called an "eye-opening experience" as she came to understand more about them. Additionally, many of the workers were not used to seeing a woman in training on the factory floor, so she was initially exposed to catcalls. She addressed the workers about the reasons they were doing this, and they soon ceased these actions.

Mary also learned about how fast-changing markets affect sales. The oil crisis during 1979–80 had increased gasoline prices to new highs, resulting in plummeting car sales. Then came the rapid growth of the Japanese car market during the 1980s and '90s. Representatives of the Big Three had predicted it would reach no more than 10 percent of the market, but it eventually expanded to a significant one-third of the market when the Japanese began producing more fuel-efficient and reliable cars than the Big Three.

All these events and more continued unfolding while Mary was studying at GMI. However, unlike the majority of women studying there, who were majoring in industrial administration, she majored in electrical engineering, which required her to complete more technical courses. She selected that major because it involved more math and because her drafting skills, which were required for some other majors, were not her strongest area.

As did the other students studying at GMI, she alternated between working on-site at a GM location and studying, with no summers off or spring breaks. She continued earning wages while studying and also had savings from her high school job at Felice's grocery store. As a lover of cars, she first attempted to put a down payment on the purchase of a red Firebird. However, she settled on a red Chevrolet Chevette once she determined that she could not continue to pay for school and afford a more expensive car.

In their second year of studying at GMI, students began supervising workers who were often twice their age. Through this experience, they often learned toughness but also empathy and how to bond with workers in various environments and circumstances. Barra thought it was a great opportunity to learn about the "core of the business" and treating people with respect. She said that was when she became hooked on manufacturing.

After graduating from GMI in 1985, she was hired as a controls engineer at the Fiero plant, which meant she oversaw plant facilities and maintenance, including supervising plumbers, electricians and sanitation workers. This was her first true supervisory job, and when the plant had a paint shop equipment failure, she used a teamwork approach, soliciting suggestions from her team, coming up with a viable solution and impressing her boss with how she maintained her composure.

At the juncture when GM decided to close down the Fiero plant, Mary applied for and received a General Motors Fellowship to pursue her MBA from Stanford University, which would help her advance in her career when she returned to GM. She wanted to move on from supervising maintenance, but she also found that step in her career to have been valuable, and at Stanford, she learned a lot more about leadership and motivating workers. "It was all about hearts and minds," she said. She explained that when you engage people in the work they are doing, you get better results.[43]

In 1990, Mary Barra graduated from Stanford in the top 10 percent of her class and returned to GM.[44] By 1997, she had progressed from being former GM CEO Jack Smith's assistant, where she learned how GM was run at the highest levels, to working in communications. Over the years, before she became CEO, she worked in almost every area of the business. She was plant manager at the Detroit Hamtramck Assembly Plant in 2003, executive director of Vehicle Manufacturing Engineering from 2004 to 2008, vice president of Global Manufacturing Engineering from 2008 to 2009, vice president of Global Human Resources from 2009 to 2011 and senior vice president of Global Product Development from 2011 to 2013. In 2013, she was appointed executive vice president for Global Product Development, Purchasing and Supply Chain. At the end of 2013, her promotion to CEO of GM was announced, and she took the helm in January 2014. Her list of appointments continues to expand. In 2022, she was appointed to the Homeland Security Advisory Council.

Although Mary Barra might appear to be all work and no play, she admits that she enjoys making dinner with her husband, whom she met while attending GMI and later married and with whom she had two children, now grown and living out of state. She also likes reading—particularly books dealing with leadership—and "retail therapy," meaning shopping at some of Oakland County's premier department stores.

Mary Liz Curtin

Clawson

To quote from *Star Wars*, "The force is strong with this one."[45]

In person, Mary Liz Curtin, who is the co-owner of Leon & Lulu and Three Cats Restaurant in Clawson, is as dynamic and colorful as the products she offers for sale to her customers. Her award-winning "destination lifestyle store," which she opened with her husband, Stephen Scannell, in 2006, displays and sells many one-of-a-kind products ranging from upscale furniture, antiques, gourmet foods and women's clothing to unique toys, books, jewelry, small accessories and novelties. All these items are housed and artfully displayed in the former Ambassador Roller Rink building, which was built in 1941 and operated as a roller rink until 2005, when Mary Liz and Stephen purchased the building for adaptive reuse as a store.[46]

"When we decided to do this, everyone thought we were crazy," she says. "My husband searched for a building large enough for a furniture store, easily accessible from anywhere in the Detroit Metro area and with proprietary parking. The Ambassador Roller Rink fit the bill perfectly and

Right: Mary Liz Curtin with Bertie Wooster. *Courtesy of Mary Liz Curtin.*

Opposite: A furniture and gifts display at Leon & Lulu. *Courtesy of Mary Liz Curtin.*

is a magical historic building. We spent every nickel we had to buy the property, do the build-out and try to fill it. We have been profitable since our third month in business."

Mary Liz says they kept as much of the Ambassador's history as they could. They still display the trophies and skates; the rink floor is intact, complete with skate marks and practice lines; and the disco ball reigns supreme in the center. The store's entryway also showcases old photos and artifacts from skating competitions.

"No other retailer has such a depth of weirdness and breadth of product," Mary Liz says with a smile. "We love vintage items, handmade goods and things that make our customers laugh. Our commitment is to great design, fabulous service and a memorable experience."

In 2019, Mary Liz and Stephen opened Three Cats Restaurant in the former Clawson movie theater next door. "It took us five years to remodel that building. The theater closed in 1960, and by then the building had become a derelict warehouse that needed everything: a new roof, HVAC, a parking lot, electric, plumbing—everything," she says. "Our marquee is an exact replica of the 1941 original. The interior did not offer much to work with, but we have created an unusual space that recalls the movie theater as well as a wild circus. Three Cats also houses our wine and greeting card shops." In the center of the dining room, you will find a 1967 Saab two-door station wagon. The overall effect is both artsy and eclectic.

Three Cats Restaurant, originally opened with the legendary Matt Prentice as chef, serves brunch, lunch and dinner and is a popular venue

for weddings, showers and parties of all kinds. Although Matt died in 2021, his recipes and training continue to influence Three Cats. The menu, which changes seasonally, celebrates local small-batch purveyors and features scratch-made cuisine, American wines and lots of mushrooms.

Leon & Lulu and Three Cats Restaurant truly must be seen to be believed. And from the way Clawson has grown and changed over the two decades since their store opened, it appears that Mary Liz and her husband's efforts kicked off the downtown's revitalization.

Leon & Lulu is named for Mary Liz's pets, a beloved black-and-white cat called Leon Redbone and a friendly Rottweiler named Lulu, who was their first greeter. Today, Bertie Wooster, a Shih Tzu and poodle mix named for the idle-rich British gentleman in the Jeeves and Wooster stories by P.G. Wodehouse, roams the store. A pet-friendly shop, Leon & Lulu also frequently welcomes service dogs with their trainers.

Although Mary Liz is not originally from Metro Detroit, she has Midwestern roots. She was born in Chicago in 1954 and lived there until 1962, when her family moved to Santa Barbara. She attended a parochial grade school in Oak Park, Illinois, and then transferred to Marymount Santa Barbara. She then attended San Jose State University, majoring in English.

Mary Liz says she inherited some of her retail savvy and love of business from her parents, particularly from her mother, Bert, who was a retailer and interior designer, in addition to having served in the U.S. Marines during World War II as an air traffic controller at Parris Island. Her father served in the U.S. Navy, and Mary Liz maintains that he is one of the reasons the United States won the war.

By the time Mary Liz turned thirty-five, she had extensive wholesale experience in both sales and management. She met Stephen Scannell, who operated Cargo Hold, a retail mainstay in Birmingham, Michigan, for twenty-six years, at a trade show in Chicago. When they married in 1989, Mary Liz moved permanently to Detroit, where she started Mary Liz Curtin & Company, a consultancy with clients such as eBay, Yankee Candle and many emerging vendors.

Given her college background in English and her later experience in retail and interior design, it is no surprise that Mary Liz also became a professional speaker and writer, sharing her retail and marketing expertise nationally in person and in writing for publications such as *The Wall Street Journal*, *Gifts and Dec*, *Floral Management* and *Giftware News*. Additionally, she wrote a book titled *A Shopkeeper's Manual* that was published in 2006, which is filled with clear, practical information about how to achieve retail success.

"I love display, and we both love product," she says. "We're a great match, and we've made Leon & Lulu a fun place to shop. People come here who are feeling down in order to feel better. We want our customers to leave smiling whether they have made a purchase or not."

Mary Liz and Stephen have two children, Keara and Kegan, who both work at Leon & Lulu. Like her mother, Keara is energetic and creative, and she works as a performer. Known as Tumbleweed, she is a roller-skating, fire-spinning, juggling, stilt-walking clown and the brand ambassador for Leon & Lulu. She also performs internationally at festivals, parties and other events. Kegan is in charge of all things technical, building maintenance and crisis management of all kinds.

Mary Liz has won several awards since Leon & Lulu opened in Clawson, not only for her retail savvy but also for the charity work she does to help develop emerging artists and writers. These include a Michiganian of the Year Award, an Oakland County Commendation from the Board of Commissioners, several ARTS and Retail Excellence Awards, a Global Innovation Award for Retail Excellence and an ICON award. "Four times a year, we have the Michigan-made market that displays and sells the work of local artists," she says. "Plus we embrace multiple charities, including Animal Rescue, Oakland Literacy, We Care Foster Care, the Judson Center and more. In fact, we built our business so that we could contribute to charities, and we have done many benefits." Leon & Lulu hosts about seventy events a year, most of them charity-oriented.

Chapter 3
PUBLIC OFFICIALS

Hilda Gage (1939–2010)

BLOOMFIELD HILLS

Hilda Gage achieved many firsts in the legal field during her lifetime, and she is thus remembered by her colleagues as a pioneer in the legal field. She was the first female chief judge of Michigan's Oakland County Circuit Court—a court that has been deemed "one of the busiest circuit courts in the nation."[47] She was also the first woman president of the Michigan Judges Association and the first woman to chair the American Bar Association's National Conference of State Trial Judges.

Hilda achieved all this and more despite having multiple sclerosis, which forced her to retire from her position on the Michigan Court of Appeals, where she served from 1997 to 2006. Later in her life, she was also diagnosed with Parkinson's disease.[48] "She thought of [her health issues] as an inconvenience. It did not stop her," said her sister-in-law Judy Rosenberg.[49]

Oakland Circuit Judge Edward Sosnick said that Hilda was a "wonder woman." "She never lost her ability to laugh at herself or failed to reach out—even if her hands were shaking—when a person or group sought out her talents." Judge Sosnick also said that Hilda was noted for being kind to young lawyers.[50]

Hilda was born in 1939 in Detroit to Jacob and Mildred Rosenberg and was the youngest of three children. After graduating from Mumford High School in 1957, she earned a bachelor's degree in constitutional history,

Oakland County Circuit Judge Hilda Gage, 1986. © *Detroit Free Press/USA TODAY NETWORK.*

with distinction, from the University of Michigan (UM) in 1960. She followed that with a master's in elementary education in 1962, also from UM. However, she discovered that she enjoyed working with her husband, Noel Gage, on briefing cases while he attended law school—so much so that she chose to study for a law degree herself. With two children at that time, she decided to attend night school at Wayne State University (WSU) Law School. After earning her law degree magna cum laude, she stayed on for a couple of years at WSU to teach legal research. Then she joined a Detroit law firm with clients that included Detroit Edison, the Detroit Board of Education, boxing champion Leon Spinks and singer Aretha Franklin. "There weren't many women lawyers at the time, and I was afforded the opportunity to handle just about anything," she said. "We had an interesting caseload and some high-profile clients."[51]

In 1974, Hilda was diagnosed with MS, and that same year, she also lost her six-and-a-half-year-old son, Robbie, to dysautonomia—a disorder of the autonomic nervous system. "He had been hospitalized thirty-three times...and died in his sleep at home. It was a tragedy that a parent can't put into words," she said.[52] She would later also lose her daughter, Jackie, to the same disorder.

After four years in private practice, Hilda returned to WSU in 1977 to teach a course titled Contemporary Issues Affecting Consumers: The Family and the Law.[53] Then, in 1978, she was elected to the Oakland County Circuit Court bench. She served there through 1996. One of her highest-profile decisions as a circuit court judge was her ruling that a quadriplegic who had petitioned the court for his right to die had the right to refuse medical treatment.[54]

From the circuit court, she moved to the Michigan Court of Appeals, to which she was twice elected. Due to health reasons, she resigned in 2006. "She is both a great judge and a great lady," Chief Judge William Whitbeck said at the time. "Uncompromising legal scholarship, amazing grace, tremendous strength of character, and enormous courage—that is Judge Hilda Gage. Her standards are high, but never more so than when she applies them to herself."[55]

Hilda's sister-in-law, Judy Rosenberg, said that she believed Hilda just liked helping people, being involved in justice and bringing fairness to people. During her lifetime, Hilda also served on the executive boards of the National Multiple Sclerosis Society and the Michigan Children's Hospital. She also cofounded Michigan's chapter of the Dysautonomia Foundation.[56] In 1995, she was inducted into the Michigan Women's Hall of Fame, and a year later, she was named Michiganian of the Year for her excellence and dedication to charitable work.[57]

Hilda Gage died in Las Vegas on September 13, 2010, age seventy-one, from complications of multiple sclerosis. She was survived by her daughter Julie Gage Palmer; her husband, John Palmer; and three grandchildren.

Her daughter Julie followed in her mother's footsteps: she became an attorney, taught at the University of Chicago Law School and wrote a book on genetics. Hilda also coauthored a well-received book titled *The Judge's Book*.

IN HER OWN WORDS

Saving the Barton Farmhouse

By Pat Hardy

Pat Hardy. *Courtesy of Pat Hardy.*

An accomplished and admired writer friend of mine once wrote, "Pat Hardy can move mountains!"—whereupon I countered her adamantly, "No, I can't! I've only moved one historic house, and I didn't do it alone." My correction wasn't meant as a reprimand. It was merely a statement of fact, for as a former mayor and city commissioner in Bloomfield Hills, I saw myself as a catalyst, willing to get any ball rolling, no matter what position I held, if there were others willing to help.

In the matter of "Saving the Historic Barton Farmhouse," the oldest existing pre–Civil War farmhouse in the City of Bloomfield Hills, it was Harry C. Walsh, a revered area realtor, who alerted me to the potential loss of such a valuable part of the city's history, especially during the celebration of the city's seventy-fifth anniversary in 2008. Harry contacted me, the mayor at that time, out of sheer desperation, knowing that the demolition was close at hand. The home and lush property on Long Lake Road had been acquired by Mancini Brothers, developers who planned to build luxury homes on the prestigious Bloomfield Hills site. Harry learned that there were no plans to incorporate the house into their upscale vision, and he was at his wits' end. He urged the city to order an immediate cease and desist.

Harry took me to see the house with its "dirt floor" Michigan basement and original glass windows, flooring and moldings, and I understood his concern. I immediately contacted fellow commissioner Dave Kellett, a renowned builder and history buff. He confirmed it was a rare, authentic Greek Revival home, probably built around 1832, according to Harry's records and those of Connie and Carl O. Barton, who bought the charming little white farmhouse in 1938. There were not that many homes like it left in Michigan.

With Kellett's validation, I then approached Jay Cravens, our city manager, and the rest of the five-person city commission to join an effort to save the house. It was decided to contact other entities who could benefit from saving the house for educational and community use. The first joint meeting of the entire boards of the City of Bloomfield Hills, the Charter Township of Bloomfield, the Bloomfield Hills School District and the Bloomfield Historical Society was quickly arranged to determine if there was a consensus to work together to accomplish such a tremendous task. It was a first-time coalition of those boards, which eventually became known as the Four B's.

During that meeting, two representatives from each of the B's and one public liaison were elected to form a study committee to determine how much community interest there might be in going forward. I invited several friends to my home to see if they would help generate awareness and funds to help in the effort. Thus, the eventual bodies of the Board of Preservation Bloomfield and its fundraising arm, the Friends of Preservation Bloomfield, arose, raising over time the massive sum of more than $1 million during extremely difficult financial times via two appeal letters and various popular yearly fundraisers: Antique and Treasure Sales, B-Hive Balls, Gingerbread House Brunches, Corn Roasts, Fashion Shows, Historic Home Open Houses, Fisher Theatre Evenings and many other smaller gatherings.

If it were not for the immediate seed money of $50,000 generously donated by the Barton sisters, Margy and Mary; Mancini Brothers'

The Barton Farmhouse during its move from Long Lake Road to the Bowers School Farm on Square Lake Road. *Photograph by and courtesy of John Marshall.*

agreement to sell the house for the sum of $1 (accompanied by their donation of $10,000); several major donors; many pro bono donors; countless fundraisers; and the willingness of the Bloomfield Hills School District to include the house on land allocated for an educational park on the grounds of the Bowers School Farm (designed for educational and community use, a perfect spot for the farmhouse), this amazing feat would never have been accomplished.

A plaque mounted at the side entrance to the farmhouse lists the major donors who, in 2008, made "Saving the Historic Barton Farmhouse" possible. A history book is in the works listing all donors, large and small, who made a financial contribution of five dollars or more in 2008 to preserve the house as a lasting testament to what can be achieved, despite the worst economic conditions, when people work together for a common purpose.

During my lifetime, I have been involved in many causes and have received much recognition for my involvement, but the greatest reward has always been the many friendships made during both happy

The historic Barton Farmhouse on the Bowers School Farm, 2024. *Author's collection.*

and difficult times. I credit my attorney husband, Tom Hardy, for supporting each successful endeavor (as well as those where I missed the mark) during our sixty-three-year marriage. The only thing he ever mandated was that I be home when the four Hardy Girls—Lisa, Lanie, Leslie and Liz—came home from school. As a youngster, he begrudged the fact that his mother, Betty Harp, a legendary retailer and founder of Harp's Lingerie, was always working. She couldn't be home with cookies and milk on the table when Tom and his brother came home, as much as they and she might have wished. His support of my endeavors has been crucial, inspiring and essential. Surely, Tom Hardy has been the greatest blessing of my life. I never would have become the person I am today without him.

Chapter 4

PHYSICIANS AND SCIENTISTS

Dr. Bertha Van Hoosen (1863–1952)

ROCHESTER HILLS

Before Dr. Bertha Van Hoosen perfected the buttonhole appendectomy, patients who needed their appendix removed would have a larger incision made, which could result in complications and a longer recovery time.[58] Another one of Dr. Van Hoosen's innovations in the medical field was her experimentation with and development of scopolamine-morphine anesthesia, or "twilight sleep," which anesthetized patients without "inhibiting their reflexes."[59] This type of anesthesia was particularly useful for women during childbirth.

During Bertha's lifetime, she became one of the best-known and longest-practicing women physicians in medical history. Her achievements spilled over into high-level medical leadership roles. In 1918, she became the first woman to head a medical division of a coeducational university as professor and head of obstetrics at Loyola University.[60] She achieved this pinnacle despite the sexual discrimination she had to battle throughout her career, as women physicians were a rarity during her lifetime and found it difficult to be accepted as capable by their male peers. No matter the discriminatory challenges she faced, she remained dedicated to women's health issues as well as to the education and training of other women physicians.[61]

Bertha Van Hoosen as a young woman. *From the Archives of the Rochester Hills Museum at Van Hoosen Farm.*

Bertha was once referred to as the "red-headed dynamo" due to the "spirited manner" with which she pursued a career in medicine. Her life began quietly on her family's farm in Stoney Creek, Michigan.[62] She was born there on March 26, 1863, the second of two daughters of Joshua Van Hoosen, a farmer, and his wife, Sarah Ann Taylor, a teacher. The land on which Bertha grew up is now part of the Rochester Hills Museum at Van Hoosen Farm complex in Rochester Hills. She would say her education began when she was a young girl living on that farm, "her hundred-acre backyard playground, where procreation, birth, and death were a natural part of everyday life."[63]

After attending a one-room schoolhouse during their elementary years, Bertha and her sister, Alice, attended high school in Pontiac, which was twelve miles from their home. During the week, the sisters boarded with families in Pontiac, but for the weekend, they would be picked up by horse and buggy, driven home and then redelivered to the school early on Monday.[64]

Bertha was an excellent student, skipping several grades. Following her graduation in 1880, she attended the University of Michigan (UM), initially studying literature. However, after meeting and talking with other young women who were attending the university's medical school, she became excited by the idea of becoming a doctor herself. When she told her parents what she was thinking, they disapproved and instead insisted she become a teacher or stay on the farm. Bertha, however, remained steadfast. When her father stopped funding her education because she would not give up her dream of being a doctor, Bertha worked a variety of jobs to earn the money needed to pay her tuition.[65] She also took only those classes she thought would create a solid, acceptable premed program. Bertha was successful and graduated with a BA from UM in 1884. She continued her studies at UM and graduated from its medical school in 1888.

Once she began working as a doctor, she suffered a great deal of sexual discrimination in the almost exclusively male field of medicine. She persevered once again, and in 1892, she established a successful private medical practice of her own in Chicago, specializing in obstetrics, gynecology and surgery. In 1911, she was inducted into the University of Michigan's Hall of Fame.

Bertha went on to hold prestigious positions on many hospital staffs and university faculties and founded the American Medical Women's Association in 1915, becoming its first president.[66] Throughout the years, she also mentored many other women who hoped to become physicians and surgeons, always referring to them with affection as her "surgical daughters."

Dr. Bertha Van Hoosen received numerous honors and accolades during her lifetime, all of which are chronicled in her highly praised autobiography *Petticoat Surgeon*, which was published in 1947. That same year, she was made an honorary member of the International Association of Medical Women—only the second woman in history, after Marie Curie, to receive that distinction.[67]

During her lifetime, Dr. Van Hoosen delivered thousands of babies, and she continued operating into her eighties, even after losing one finger, which she said made her hand "smaller and more agile" for operating.[68] She had become the most famous woman physician of her time and claimed she would know exactly when it was time for her to retire. In 1952, she suffered a stroke, and she died in June that same year.

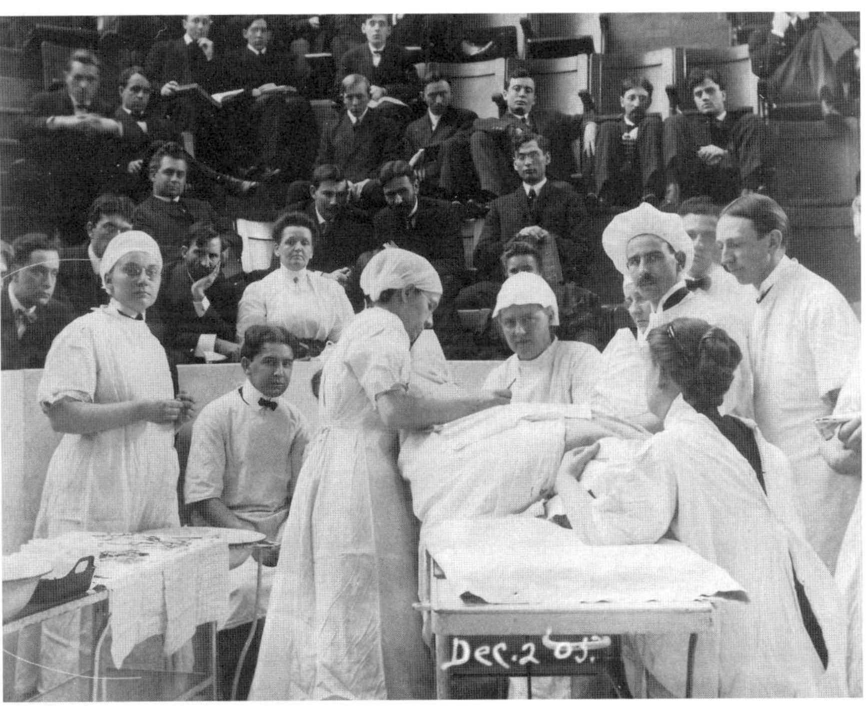

Dr. Bertha Van Hoosen overseeing an operation. *From the Archives of the Rochester Hills Museum at Van Hoosen Farm.*

According to Maureen Thalmann, author of the 2015 book *Petticoat Surgeon: The Extraordinary Life of Dr. Bertha Van Hoosen*, Bertha wrote near the end of her life, "When I was born, the door that separates the sexes had opened scarcely more than a crack, but it has been my privilege, my pain, and my pleasure to pound on that door…and finally to see it, although not wide open, stand ajar."[69]

Dr. Petra Huck

CRANBROOK INSTITUTE OF SCIENCE

On any given day at Cranbrook Institute of Science (CIS) in Bloomfield Hills, visitors will likely come upon the large skeleton of a *Tyrannosaurus rex*, interactive displays about the solar system and holograms of scientists explaining ancient artifacts, among other compelling exhibits. But they will also encounter information about women achievers in STEAM (Science, Technology, Engineering, Arts and Mathematics). One of the women featured is Dr. Petra Huck, an atmospheric scientist who specializes in research about the ozone hole and climate change and who is also a wife, a mother and a science educator at CIS.[70]

Dr. Huck became a research scientist in 2011, after her second daughter was born. With her infant daughter in a baby carrier, she presented her research at the WCRP Open Science Conference in 2011 in Denver, Colorado, and for that presentation, she received the award for Outstanding Presentation Among Early Career and Young Scientists. She has continued doing ozone and climate research and has received more than $360,000 in research grants. She has also contributed to two international environmental reports and published eight articles in international scientific journals. Additionally, she has made twenty-five conference contributions.

Petra Huck was born in Freiburg, Germany, in 1976 to Christine and Klaus Huck. She grew up in Grenzach-Wyhlen, a small German town on the border of Switzerland and France where her grandparents also lived. In fact, when she looked out of her bedroom window, she could see Switzerland. For elementary and high school, she attended the local schools in Grenzach-Wyhlen. As a young girl, she most enjoyed reading, being outdoors and observing animals. "My favorite classes were always about science," she has said, "but by the time I was in high school, I was hooked on chemistry."

Dr. Petra Huck receiving her PhD. *Courtesy of Dr. Petra Huck.*

A top student, Petra won awards every year for her academic achievements. "I really liked going to school and learning, and I found it easy." However, in high school, she was still unsure what she wanted to be. All she knew was that she did not want a nine-to-five office job because she preferred to be outdoors so much.

Then, in the eleventh grade, she became a foreign exchange student and lived with a host family in Phoenix, Arizona. "That was a wonderful time for me," she has said. "I felt particularly free being in the U.S., and I wanted to return."

Toward the end of high school in Germany, she studied possible careers using a computer program set up for graduates to help them learn about different career paths. Based on this information, graduates could begin to narrow down the fields they liked and disliked. Her first choice came up repeatedly: meteorologist. She wholeheartedly agreed. "That's it—that's what I want to be!" Once she knew her career target, she determined the prerequisites for study, one of which was physics. Although it was not her strength, she knew she had to pursue it.

She also thought that she should learn more English and practice it firsthand, so after high school, she came to the United States and worked as an au pair for a family in Atlanta. That family also encouraged her to pursue a college education. She remembers the father, who was a graduate of Princeton University, and the mother, who had earned a master's degree in theater and performance studies from Georgia State University, telling her, "You can do it!" To this day, she remains friends and stays in touch with that family. And yes, she did go to college. In fact, she was the first in her family to attend.

After returning to Germany, Petra enrolled at the University of Karlsruhe, but to her surprise, she failed her first-year math exams. "This experience made me doubt myself, and I wondered whether I was studying in the right field and even at the right school." She said that in Germany, students are left more on their own than students in the United States to succeed or fail, and universities typically lose about 50 percent of first-year students this way, weeding out those who are not suited for a major or do not know how to study. However, Petra remained determined, and she also had good friends who encouraged her not to quit after only the first try. From this experience, Petra learned two important lessons. First, she learned how to study harder, and second, she learned how to fail before trying again and achieving success. She has said that both are important lessons for everyone to learn in life.

Petra did stay enrolled at the university, and on her second attempt, she passed the exams. Nonetheless, she continued to find math difficult and to doubt herself at times. However, she couldn't think of any other field she really wanted to work in, so she stuck with her studies. After she passed her pre-diploma exams two years in, her classes became smaller, often with only eight students in them. These classes focused on climatology and meteorology, her areas of keen interest, and she began to do well again.

In 2001, one of her professors suggested she do research on sediment-laden sea ice in the Arctic for a project taking place in Fairbanks, Alaska. She was accepted for the project, and once there, she conducted research and wrote a paper about her findings. For her master's thesis, she researched the polar ozone, which had been one of the biggest concerns in climate research since the ozone hole discovery in the 1980s. She has said that the Montreal Protocol, a treaty that 198 nations signed in 1987 to ban ozone-depleting substances, is indeed working. "Today, ozone-depleting substances are still decreasing, and although it will take one hundred years or more for the ozone layer to recover, it will return to pre-1980 levels." However, she concedes that there is much more work to be done in other areas concerning the climate. In 2003, Petra received the equivalent of an MS in meteorology from the University of Karlsruhe Institute of Meteorology and Climate Research. She went on to study for her PhD at the University of Canterbury in Christchurch, New Zealand. In 2005, she became a visiting PhD student at the National Center of Atmospheric Research in Boulder, Colorado. Later that year, she married her high school sweetheart, who had also gone on to study at the University of Canterbury, receiving his PhD in engineering. During this same year, she continued to conduct research on the ozone and climate and began publishing in international reports and journals.

In 2007, she earned her PhD in atmospheric physics from the University of Canterbury; her dissertation focused on the coupling of dynamics and chemistry in the Antarctic stratosphere. Since her husband was also pursuing further studies in New Zealand, they both remained there until 2012 before returning to Europe. She conducted postdoctoral research on the ozone hole and climate change through the National Institute of Water and Atmospheric Research (NIWA) after receiving a German Research Association grant.

Over the years, Petra gave birth to three daughters and enjoyed being a "100 percent mom" for some time. When her daughters were all of school age, she and her husband applied to homeschool them, a request the German government allowed since both parents had a PhD. "However, my husband and I decided to world school our children, so we took them on a one-year trip, visiting twenty-three countries across five continents!" Then, in 2021, her husband accepted a position in Michigan as the president of an international company.

One day, while her husband was at work, Petra visited the Cranbrook Institute of Science and was immediately impressed. She volunteered there at first and became a museum educator a year later, teaching children science through outreach programs, a role she enjoys. Indeed, she does teach them about climate change but also about all kinds of science typically of keen interest to children, such as dinosaurs and insects, as well as about scientific thinking. Additionally, she actively works with Women Rock Science, and it is she who put together the information displayed at CIS about the accomplishments of women in science.

Petra and her husband currently reside in Oakland County with their three daughters. She says that it is still tough for working women with young children. That is, they cannot be Mom 100 percent, and they cannot be 100 percent dedicated to their profession. She believes that if it were to become more acceptable to allow small children to be present with their mothers at work sometimes, we would see more professional achievements by women.

Chapter 5

AUTHORS AND ARTISTS

Anne Morrow Lindbergh (1906–2001)

BLOOMFIELD HILLS

Anne Morrow Lindbergh was an author, an aviator and the wife of Charles Lindbergh, the world-famous pilot who was the first to fly solo across the Atlantic Ocean from New York to Paris. She and Charles lived in Oakland County for only a couple of years during World War II while he worked at Willow Run as a technical consultant. During that time, the couple leased a house on Cranbrook Road near Woodward Avenue in Bloomfield Hills. It was there that Anne Morrow Lindbergh wrote her first novel, *The Steep Ascent*, in a trailer behind the house. According to Charles's diary, he often joined her in this same trailer to write, and his entries eventually were incorporated into the books *The Spirit of St. Louis* and *The Wartime Journals of Charles A. Lindbergh*. Both Anne's and Charles's books would go on to be published by Harcourt Brace during different decades.[71]

Anne Spencer Morrow was born in Englewood, New Jersey, on June 22, 1906, and grew up there. Her father was Dwight Morrow, a prominent banker. During the mid-1920s, she attended Smith College, majoring in English. In 1927, while she was on Christmas break from college, she attended an embassy reception in Mexico City, where her father was serving as the U.S. ambassador. It was there that she met Charles Lindbergh, the

Anne Morrow Lindbergh preparing to fly with her husband, Charles Lindbergh. *Courtesy of Wikimedia Commons.*

guest of honor, who was on his Latin American tour and already world-famous for his solo flight across the Atlantic Ocean.

To attend the reception, Charles had flown alone to Mexico in poor weather over 2,100 miles. When he arrived in Mexico, more than 150,000 people were there to greet him as a hero and the world's most eligible bachelor.[72] During the next year, Charles courted Anne, even giving her flying lessons. In 1928, Anne graduated from Smith College with honors, and on May 27, 1929, at age twenty-three, she married Charles Lindbergh. That same year, she also became the first American woman to earn a glider pilot's license.

Anne said that even before she married Charles Lindbergh, he had already given her a confidence she had not had before. "The man I was to marry believed in me and what I could do, and consequently I found that I could do more than I realized."[73]

A little more than a year later, Anne gave birth to the first of six children she would have with Charles. They named the baby Charles Augustus Lindbergh III. Then, beginning in 1931, she flew as copilot with her husband in a single-engine plane on historic flights across the world. She and Charles flew north across Canada and Alaska and on to China and Japan, with Anne serving as the radio operator. Based on their experiences on this trip, she wrote her first nonfiction book, titled *North to the Orient*.

However, in March 1932, tragedy struck when the couple's firstborn son, Charles, was kidnapped and murdered, resulting in what many newspapers and legal scholars called the "trial of the century." Due to the sensationalism of the trial, as well as threats made against the life of their second son, Jon, the Lindberghs sought refuge by moving to Europe in 1935.

Cover of *The Steep Ascent. Author's collection.*

With Europe at war in 1939, the Lindberghs returned to the United States to live. By 1942, Charles was working as a technical consultant for Henry Ford at Willow Run to help switch U.S. automobile plants over to bomber production. That same year, Anne and her children joined Charles in Bloomfield Hills to live in the first of two furnished houses they would rent during 1942–43. It was while living for one year in the home on Cranbrook Road just west of Woodward that Anne began to write her first novel.[74]

The Lindberghs rented the 1923 Albert Khan–designed house from owner Kathleen Belknap, who during that period called it Belwood.[75] To comfort Anne, who was pregnant and having trouble sleeping in her new home, Charles purchased and brought home a trailer as a sort of "permanent movable workroom" for her and placed it in the backyard woods.[76] This delighted Anne, who called it "quiet, compact, and neat…[with] a table and windows the right height at which to write."[77]

Charles also liked the idea of the trailer for another reason: it could quickly become a movable form of shelter for the family during an uncertain period. Due to the rubber shortage at that time and the possibility of theft, he removed the trailer's tires and stored them in the home's basement.

On August 12, 1942, Anne gave birth to their son Scott, and within weeks, she began feeling comfortable in her new home. She had already been welcomed to the neighborhood by Carolyn Farr Booth, wife of Henry Scripps Booth, and she soon met more neighbors and became friends with Kate Thompson Bromley, who lived across Cranbrook Road, where the Congregational Church of Birmingham now stands. Over time, she and Charles also began to meet more of the people who were working at

Anne Morrow Lindbergh with her son Charles Jr., her mother and her grandmother. *Courtesy of Wikimedia Commons.*

Cranbrook and enjoyed dinners at the homes of Mr. and Mrs. Carl Milles and Eliel and Loja Saarinen.

By Christmas 1942, the Lindberghs felt completely at home at Belwood: Anne wrote about hearing the church bells of Christ Church Cranbrook ringing carols in the distance, and Charles described that Christmas Eve as "the best…we have ever had."[78] He also wrote in his diary about working on his *Spirit of St. Louis* manuscript and described the many walks that he and Anne enjoyed along Cranbrook Road and through the grounds of the Cranbrook community itself.[79]

During January 1943, Anne went to the trailer every day to write, and she described Charles writing there as well when he was home, although he sometimes wrote at a card table in the living room. All the while, she continued to note the effects of the war; on February 10, 1943, she wrote in her diary that shoes and meat were being rationed.

Despite these conditions, Anne wrote less than two weeks later that she felt "changed" and did not want to return home to the East Coast. She also noted that her novel was nearly done and that she'd put into it everything she'd learned over the years. She reasoned that the Alps she described in her story, with their high peaks and abysses, might represent the mental and moral struggles many people face during their lifetimes.

In the months that followed, Anne enrolled in sculpture and art history classes at Cranbrook Academy of Art while continuing to work on her novel. On July 19, 1943, she wrote in her diary that she was looking at houses with Mr. Snyder, a realtor, because Belwood was being sold. From July 28 to August 18, 1943, nonplussed by the fact that her family would soon need to move, Anne wrote with great excitement about her blossoming creative life at Cranbrook, where she was studying sculpting with Janet DeCoux and art history with Ernst Scheyer. She described her joy at working in a studio, attending art exhibitions and having conversations with like-minded people about art, books, writing and music: "All kinds of things have begun to flower around me. Friends, all kinds—all at once. After feeling alone and dreary for so long, suddenly to find that I am not alone, that people love me, and that there are people who speak the same language. It is almost too much."[80]

By the end of August 1943, the Lindberghs had moved into their second and final rental home, which was on Goodhue Road in Bloomfield Hills. They took their trailer with them. Anne enjoyed her friendships in the area until she and her family moved back to the East Coast in 1944. She would write later that she missed her friends at Cranbrook and felt only "half alive" since she left.[81]

Although Ann had written most of her novel *The Steep Ascent* in the trailer behind their home on Cranbrook Road, the book itself was not published until March 1944. Initial sales of her book were so good that on March 30, 1944, Anne was notified by publisher Donald Brace of Harcourt Brace & World that twenty-three thousand more copies were already being printed.

After World War II, Anne and her family moved back to the East Coast permanently but returned to the Detroit area from time to time to visit Charles's mother in Grosse Pointe. Anne went on to write several more books, including her best-known work, *Gift from the Sea*, published in 1955, which became a national nonfiction bestseller. In 1979, she was inducted into the National Aviation Hall of Fame. In the 1990s, she was inducted into the National Women's Hall of Fame and the International Women in Aviation Pioneer Hall of Fame. She also received honorary degrees from five colleges, including a master's and a doctor of letters degree from Smith College, her alma mater.

Two of Anne's books, *North to the Orient* and *Listen! The Wind*, won the National Book Award, while her published diaries, *War Within and Without*, which included entries about her life in Bloomfield Hills, won the Christopher Award.

After a series of strokes in the 1990s, Anne Lindbergh went to live in a house on her daughter Reeve's property in Passumpsic, Vermont. In 2001, at age ninety-four, she died there. Charles Lindbergh had died years earlier at age seventy-two in Hawaii from lymphoma. His book, *The Spirit of St. Louis*, which was published in 1953, had won the Pulitzer Prize in 1954.

Nora Chapa Mendoza

WEST BLOOMFIELD

Nora Chapa Mendoza is an "artist's artist," meaning she is an artist who is highly respected by other artists, gallerists and museum curators. She is dedicated to her profession and makes art every single day because, she says, painting is like eating for her. She has no choice but to create; this is her passion, her life. Over a lifetime of ninety-two years, that passion has earned her numerous accolades and awards, including for her contribution to the renovation of Detroit's Music Hall in 1996, alongside eight other artists. In 1999, she was named Michigan Artist of the Year. More recently, in October 2023, she became the first Latina woman invited to "sign the beam" in Detroit's historical Scarab Club. With this monumental achievement, Nora joined the ranks of renowned local and international artists who signed the beam in past years, including Diego Rivera, Marcel Duchamp, Norman Rockwell, Shirley Woodson and Isamu Noguchi, to name just a few. "Putting my name up there, I mean, up there with Diego, that's tops!" she said. "It doesn't get much better."[82]

Nora Chapa Mendoza, 2024 Kresge Eminent Artist. *Photo by and courtesy of Laurie Psarianos.*

But it did get better. In April 2024, Nora received an honorary doctorate of the arts from Oakland University for her many accomplishments in the art field. In December the same year, she was named the 2024 Kresge Eminent Artist, Metro Detroit's premier honor for a lifetime of achievement and contributions to the region's cultural community. This award is presented annually to an artist who has lived and worked for a significant number of years in Wayne, Oakland or Macomb County, and it "celebrates artistic innovation, rewarding integrity and depth of vision with unrestricted support of $100,000."[83]

Nora's home and studio are filled with both her own artwork and her collection of fellow artists' work. Among this art, her walls are covered with plaques and framed awards, letters and tributes she has received over the years. She says that nothing makes her happier than making art—except for her two children, Laurie Psarianos and Dr. Sam Mendoza, whom she calls her "two masterpieces."[84]

In her large studio—once her home's two-car garage, which she converted and expanded—the floor is a kaleidoscope of splashed and dripped colors, somewhat reminiscent of a large Jackson Pollock drip painting. Hundreds of acrylic and oil paintings, collages and assemblages fill the studio space. It is clear that she works daily at making art.[85] Some of her most prominent pieces, created earlier in her life, are still displayed in this space, perhaps not for much longer. These signature pieces are likely to end up in museums or private collections.

One such work, titled *Fire Ants*, depicts a crying toddler on a Texas-shaped surface with three large ants attached to it. This piece is a memory of her pain when, as a crying child, she was placed outdoors on the ground in an attempt to make her stop crying, which instead only made her cry more because she was soon being bitten by ants.[86]

Later in her career, her abstract work often introduced unexpected visual elements, surprising her viewers. For example, in her abstract titled *Wild Horses*, an image of a running horse emerges from swirling colors.[87] Nora conceived this painting with memories of her grandfather, Arcadio Chapa, a horse trainer who died while attempting to tame a particularly wild horse.

Nora's signature mixed-media painting, *Metamorphosis*, poignantly illustrates her transformation into a new life following her divorce in 1975. In the painting, Nora manifests her genuine self as she discovers that her true marriage, her unmistakable calling, is making art. This strong painting includes hidden images of Nora's past, many symbolic, with powerful messages. The viewer may peek through a keyhole in the woman's gown to read Nora's message revealing the past suffering she endured.[88] The image of this painting was licensed by CBS and can be seen on the set of *Walker*, the new version of *Walker, Texas Ranger*.

Nora Chapa was born on January 20, 1932, in Weslaco, Texas, in the heart of the Rio Grande Valley close to the Mexican border. She is very proud of her Mexican and Indigenous heritage. Nora's parents, Casimiro and Josefa Chapa, were both in their twenties and struggling financially when she was born. They lived in a one-room house, and money perpetually remained tight. When Nora's mother died four years after her birth, her father left his three children in the care of an aunt who already had many children of her own.

Nora remembers well the struggles of her family's early life, including family members picking citrus and cotton in the hot Texas sun. In the biography of Nora produced by the Kresge Foundation, titled *Su Arte, Su Vida: Nora Chapa Mendoza*, she says, "I remember after my mother's death, my aunt tied a potato sack to me, one in front and one on my back, and took me to pick cotton with her."[89]

Nora's agricultural work delayed her schooling until she was eight years old. She struggled when she first attended school, but then she began learning English and quickly caught up. She believes it was during this period that she first became interested in art, intrigued by the colorful Mexican calendars and comic books she saw.[90] But by this time, her aunt was weary of trying to raise so many children on her own, and she returned Nora and her siblings to their father, saying, "Here's your children: you raise them."[91]

The children's return to their father proved fortuitous. Casimiro Chapa was a house painter, and he used his paints to demonstrate to Nora how to mix colors. He also encouraged her interest in making art. When Nora was fourteen, he bought her a "set of paints, a canvas, brushes, and a picture to copy."[92] She knew from that day forward that she wanted to be an artist, but in reality, many years would pass before she could truly call herself an artist. "I painted all the time. I copied everything I liked, teaching myself how to paint by painting….I didn't know any artists other than my art teacher; there were no role models for me."[93]

After high school, Nora's boyfriend discouraged her from attending college. He wanted to marry her, and he wanted a stay-at-home wife and mother. Any painting she did would have to be limited to the basement and remain a mere hobby.

In 1953, when Nora was twenty-one, the couple married and moved to Detroit, where her husband began a medical residency at Highland Park General Hospital. Nora soon gave birth to her daughter, Laurie, and her son, Sam. Despite her love for her children, Nora grew increasingly frustrated in her controlled home environment, where she was unable to create art freely. Tensions increased, and the couple divorced in 1973. "It felt like a rebirth," she said. "My whole life changed, and it hasn't stopped."[94]

Nora went on to take art classes at the College for Creative Studies and Madonna University. She also became active in the arts community in numerous ways and was a founding member of Nuestras Artes de Michigan, the first gallery in Michigan to prominently showcase Latin American artists. In 1981, she launched her own gallery, called Galeria Mendoza. She closed the gallery after three years to focus on her own art.

Nora continues to work in all mediums, from oil and acrylic paintings to collages and assemblages made with found objects, such as stringed instruments. She says that "beauty is in everything." In earlier years, she painted figuratively; she then branched out to large abstracts in oil and acrylic, which often contain hidden images of women, landscapes and Indigenous people.

Both in her art and in her life, Nora remains true to her Mexican and Indigenous roots. In the 1980s, she became a certified elder of Kanto de la Tierra in Mesa, Arizona, and was sent as a representative of this group to many different countries. She has also been cited for continuing the "fight for labor rights for migrant and farm workers, for women's rights, and for using her art to expand awareness of Chicano history."[95]

Among the accolades Nora has received over the years, she particularly treasures a letter she received from Cesar Chavez. After they met in the 1980s, he commissioned her to produce a series of paintings, which were turned into postcards to promote and raise funds for the National Farm Association, now known as the United Farm Workers. These postcards were distributed all over the world as a fundraising effort for this cause.[96]

Nora's paintings can be found in the collections of Ford, GM, Blue Cross/Blue Shield of Michigan and CBS and in collections as far away as Egypt,

Cuba, Nicaragua and El Salvador. In addition, the Smithsonian Institution contacted her in 2018 to include her letters, notes and other papers in the Archives of American Art. Her contribution is extensive and covers the years 1963 to 2013.[97]

Despite all these successes, Nora remains grounded and devoted to art-making. "I am very honored, of course, by the Kresge award," she said. "But I must still create art every day, even if it is just a drop. It nurtures me inside."

When she's asked which is her favorite artwork, you might expect Nora to select one of her signature paintings. However, after a moment of reflection, she looks up, smiling. "The next one!" she says.[98]

Chapter 6

EDUCATORS AND ADMINISTRATORS

Annemarie Bondy Roeper (1918–2012)

BLOOMFIELD HILLS AND BIRMINGHAM

Annemarie Roeper was an educator, writer and cofounder, in 1941, with her husband, George Roeper, of the Roeper School, which today has campuses in Birmingham and Bloomfield Hills. The Roeper School remains the oldest independent school in the nation serving gifted and talented students from preschool through grade twelve. Annemarie's academic model was conceived to "recognize the power of education, choice, and self-expression, and the transformative impact these principles have on young minds."[99] She strongly believed that children have a right to grow according to their individual needs.

In an article she wrote that was published in *Educating Children for Life*, she said, "Humanity has made two promises to its children. The first is to prepare a world which accepts them and provides them with opportunities to live, grow, and create in safety. The other is to help them develop their whole beings to the fullest in every respect."[100]

In 1999, for her success in educating gifted children, Annemarie received the inaugural President's Award from the National Association for Gifted

Annemarie Bondy Roeper. *Courtesy of the Roeper School.*

Children for her lifetime of distinguished service to the field. Later, in 2003, she was awarded the Humanitarian Award by the International Center for Psycho-Social Trauma for a lifetime of service to victims of trauma, "in particular her work establishing the importance of a sense of safety to a child's development."

For many people, the ideas of safety or trauma might not be immediately associated with gifted and talented education, but for Annemarie Roeper, the association was personal. It was part of her own history. Annemarie Bondy was born in Vienna, Austria-Hungary, on August 27, 1918, and attended the Schule Marienau, a progressive boarding school near Hamburg, Germany, which her mother, Gertrud Bondy, a physician and psychoanalyst trained by Sigmund Freud, had cofounded with her husband, Max Bondy, an art historian who had been a leader in the idealistic prewar German Youth Movement. It was in this school, in 1924, that Annemarie, who was Jewish, met her future husband, George Roeper, a Protestant, who was eight years her senior. In Schule Marienau, Annemarie was exposed to an educational approach that nurtured each child intellectually, emotionally and socially.

In 1937, with the Nuremberg Laws in effect, the Nazis forced Annemarie's parents to sell their school because Jews were forbidden from educating Aryans. Annemarie became a medical student at the University of Vienna and was also accepted to study child psychoanalysis with Sigmund and Anna Freud. However, in March 1938, her higher education was curtailed due to the German invasion of Austria. Annemarie fled on the last train out of Austria to Prague before the German invasion. In 1939, the Bondy family, who had taken refuge in Switzerland, moved to the United States. They had been assisted in receiving visas by prominent educational figures in the United States who endorsed their educational methods, including reformer Dorothy Canfield Fisher, who had introduced the Montessori method in the United States, and Dorothy Thompson, a prominent journalist who in 1934 became the first American journalist expelled from Nazi Germany.

Their escape from Germany was enabled by Annemarie's fiancé, George Roeper, who had worked successfully to obtain passports for the Bondys that hid the fact that they were Jewish. George had to flee Germany himself because a former Marienau schoolmate had warned him that he was on a hit list to be shot on sight for having helped the Bondys escape. Annemarie and George married in New York City two weeks after she arrived in March 1939.

Once in the United States, George and Annemarie helped her parents establish the Windsor Mountain School, which eventually was settled in Lenox, Massachusetts. In 1941, Annemarie and George were invited by the Austrian refugee psychoanalysts Richard and Editha Sterba to direct a psychoanalytically oriented nursery school and establish a grade school in Detroit. The grade school's enrollment grew quickly in its initial location, Highland Park, and the school soon moved to the New Center area of Detroit. Within five years, the school had become so popular that the Roepers were able to purchase the former Coventry Crest estate in Bloomfield Hills, which they turned into the City and Country School of Bloomfield Hills.[101] In 1956, they converted the school to focus on gifted education; a high school was added in 1965; and in 1981, the school established a second campus in Birmingham, Michigan. In 1992, the school's name was changed to the Roeper School.

In addition to its academic offerings, the Roeper School was dedicated to an educational model of social justice, and for years, the Roepers offered bus transportation to and from Detroit and Flint to bring in students from those cities. The Roepers were early civil rights activists and formally integrated the school in 1955.

"Through their life experiences, Annemarie and George truly absorbed the lesson that life is about change, and that as educators, their most important job was to help children become emotionally and intellectually confident about embracing—or at least accommodating—change and uncertainty in their own lives," said Marcia Ruff, school historian at the Roeper School.

In 1956, the Roepers became concerned about the Cold War–driven interest in identifying gifted children, believing that the lack of knowledge about the emotional needs of such children could potentially damage their potential. The Roepers consulted with prominent scholars of gifted education, including Dr. A. Harry Passow at Teachers College, Columbia University, before converting their school to provide gifted education. Roeper thus became only the second school in the nation dedicated solely to the needs of gifted students.

The school grew over the years and became known for its curriculum in meeting the emotional and academic needs of its students. During the 1960s, Annemarie consulted with Joan Ganz Cooney on the development of *Sesame Street* and taught both undergraduate and graduate courses in gifted education at Oakland University. Then, in 1978, she and George founded the peer-reviewed journal *Roeper Review*, which is still being published by the school. That same year, Annemarie and George Roeper were each awarded an honorary doctorate from Eastern Michigan University.

The famous Roeper School domes designed by Glen Paulsen of Caudill-Rowlett & Scott and associated architects. *Author's collection.*

At age sixty-two, Annemarie retired as headmistress of the Roeper School, although she remained on the school's board of trustees. Over her lifetime, she wrote more than one hundred articles and book chapters, three scholarly books and four children's books.

The Roepers retired to Oakland, California. George died there at age eighty-one in 1992. Annemarie died at age ninety-three from pneumonia in 2012. Annemarie and George are survived by their three children, three grandchildren and seven great-grandchildren.

GENEVIEVE DOOLEY (1897–1982)

SOUTHFIELD

Some people might be surprised to learn that Lawrence Technological University (LTU) in Southfield, which was founded as Lawrence Institute of Technology in 1932 by Russell E. Lawrence in Highland Park, had full-time female leadership during both the school's formation and its first thirty years. During much of the early half of the twentieth century, the majority of faculty, students, graduates and key administrators were men—with one particularly notable exception. That woman was Genevieve Dooley, and she served as the school's first registrar as well as Russell Lawrence's bookkeeper, business officer and even as the college's representative and de facto president after Russell died a mere eighteen months after founding the college.[102]

Russell's brother, E. George Lawrence, would become president in 1934 but needed time to transition into that position, and that is when Genevieve took over the day-to-day operations. According to Dick Frederick, Lawrence Tech's public relations director from 1937 to 1976, she was the glue that kept the college going during some of its toughest early years, even working without pay initially.[103]

"Genevieve was the Rock of Gibraltar. She always was there, always knew what was going on," said Frederick. "She was particularly instrumental during those early years in keeping the school's creditors at bay."[104]

Genevieve Dooley was born in Cincinnati, Ohio, in 1897 and as a young woman moved with her sister to Detroit to find employment in the booming northern city. She was hired as secretary to Russell Lawrence, who was dean of engineering at the University of Detroit.[105] However, after the stock

Left: Genevieve Dooley, circa 1932. *Print image from the University of Detroit Mercy Archives and Special Collections, University of Detroit Mercy.*

Right: Henry Ford Plaque at LTU. *Author's collection.*

market crash of 1929 and the start of the Great Depression, the university lost paying students and enrollment plummeted. That was when Russell Lawrence took the chance to start a new engineering school by leasing the former Ford-owned training building on Woodward Avenue in Highland Park from Henry and Edsel Ford. Genevieve joined Lawrence as the school's first full-time registrar.[106]

She served officially as registrar from 1932 to 1963 and was instrumental in the university's move to Southfield in 1955 and its operations thereafter, but over the decades she contributed in many other ways to the school's and the students' success. Beyond her managerial talents, hundreds of alumni remarked about her incredibly kind and caring demeanor and the wisdom of her counsel as a trusted confidant.[107]

"You were always ready with encouragement....Thank you for your faith in me," Harold Christensen, BSME '39, wrote to her in a letter that was included among the scores of tributes presented at her retirement. By then, Christensen had become a senior engineer developing Titan III space rockets for Martin Aerospace.[108]

Another student she counseled was John Z. DeLorean, BSIE '48, a former General Motors engineer and executive who is credited with designing the first muscle car, the Pontiac GTO. He later founded the DeLorean Motor Company (DMC), whose stainless steel, gull-winged-door DMC-12 was featured in the *Back to the Future* movie trilogy.[109]

Many years after she retired, Genevieve continued to mentor young people, including me, the author of this book. She was largely responsible for my attending and finishing college at LTU, higher education not having been a priority for women in my family. When she saw that I had developed a keen interest in my English classes as well as in books and how they were designed and printed, she introduced me to her niece, an editor at Simon & Schuster, who explained publishing careers to me. I finished my degree at LTU and started working in publishing almost immediately. I went on to work for a major U.S. publishing company, traveled the world and enjoyed a wonderful, productive career because of her.[110]

Throughout her retirement years, Genevieve divided her time between homes in Michigan, New York and Florida. In 1982, at age eighty-four, she passed away peacefully in Pompano Beach. At LTU, she is remembered with both an annual award and a scholarship in her name. A photograph of her and a presentation about her contributions to the advancement of women in education were featured in a 2013 art installation called *The Woman Who Grew Hope* in the Applaud That Woman Art Show at the Florida Museum for Women Artists. Additionally, this book about the lives of remarkable women who have lived or worked in Oakland County is dedicated in her memory.[111]

IN HER OWN WORDS

Sharing Our History

By Carol Bacak-Egbo, Oakland County Parks Historian

For as long as I can remember, I have been fascinated by history—not necessarily textbook history but the history around me. In the neighborhood in Pontiac where I grew up, there was an old, old house. It was empty and falling apart. We called it the haunted house. I would stare at it and wonder who had built it, who had lived in it, where they had gone. I also wondered about who had left the pieces of a broken plate I found buried behind my garage. Who were they? Why had they buried it back there? Had they lived in my house? Who? What? When? Why? These are the questions that drive history. However, I didn't pursue a career in history, at least not at first. That was because of something my father had attached to the side of our garage: a big, old chalkboard. On a daily basis, my sister and I, as well as a few neighborhood friends, would "play school" in our backyard, and I was invariably the teacher. Later, I would often hear, "You have a gift for teaching," but it wasn't just a gift; it was a passion!

Upon graduating from the University of Michigan, I began my teaching career in the Waterford School District. I would remain there for the next forty-four years as a teacher, a social studies consultant and the director of a federal Teaching American History grant. Along the way, my career would be impacted and enriched by a variety of people and places. I sailed with Pete Seeger on his sloop *Clearwater* up the Hudson River, teaching environmental awareness. I took an eight-thousand-mile train trip around the country with

Carol Bacak-Egbo giving a history presentation. *Courtesy of Carol Bacak-Egbo.*

my son in search of America the Beautiful. I spent a summer in Tanzania on a Fulbright-Hays grant, visiting schools and studying East African history—and, most memorably, spending a sunny afternoon in the home of Tanzanian President Julius Nyerere, one of my true heroes, who, like me, had begun his career as a teacher. All these experiences broadened my world and my perspectives, and, in turn, I endeavored to do the same for those I taught, whether they were children or adults.

After many twists and turns—and a touch of serendipity—I found myself offered the opportunity to become historian for Oakland County Parks. But why would a park system need a historian? Aren't parks all about natural features like wildflowers, forests and waterways? The reality is that parks are filled with human history, from Indigenous trails that once traversed them to old foundations and fence posts, remnants of former homesteads. Knowing something of the history of a park can enrich the experience a person has there. A historian is needed to find that history and share it. This was the perfect position for me, one that required both research and public engagement—a perfect blend of history and teaching.

Since our parks span Oakland County, I became focused on the history of our county, from its Indigenous beginnings down through time. I found myself investigating Native trails, early non-Indigenous farms, Civil War widows and Pontiac wagonmakers. I became immersed in a long-term project in search of the stories of formerly

Carol shares park history with a visiting family. *Courtesy of Carol Bacak-Egbo.*

enslaved freedom seekers who utilized the Underground Railroad and found their way to our county. Best of all, I was engaged in public history and could share what I had discovered with a variety of groups in a variety of places. I found myself sharing history with three hundred people in the Buhl Mansion at Addison Oaks County Park and with ten people on a pontoon boat cruising Crooked Lake at Independence Oaks.

Oakland County is just 907 square miles in size—in Earth terms, a rather small place. But it has an endless supply of stories to uncover and share. And that old, old house in my neighborhood in Pontiac—I did, in fact, eventually find out who built it and who lived in it. But I am still working on that broken plate.

Chapter 7

FASHIONISTAS AND BEAUTY QUEENS

Rosemary Bannon

FRANKLIN

As a young assistant department manager working at Saks Fifth Avenue in 1950s Detroit, Rosemary Bannon was known as a "Chanel Girl" due to her sense of style and love of Chanel fashions. "When you know, you know," she has said about her understanding of fashion design and trends, which led to her employment with several other top high-end retailers and designers over the decades. Beyond her retail accomplishments, Rosemary made an important contribution to the history of Detroit fashion as one of the first founders and directors of the Fashion Group of Detroit. "The Detroit group was then part of the National Fashion Group, which truly launched Detroit into the 'fashion world,'" she has said. She also went on to create headline-making fashion shows and galas that raised the fashion profile of Detroit while also raising funds in support of worthwhile causes.[112]

Rosemary Bannon, who enthusiastically celebrated her ninety-fifth birthday in 2024 with many friends and her daughter, Contessa, remains as "spunky and gutsy" as back in the days when she started her fashion career. "I inherited my grandfather's energy," she said, "as he was known for this same trait. He was sort of a rebel, and so was I."

Rosemary was born in 1929 to Mr. and Mrs. Tobia Hakim, who immigrated from Lebanon to Detroit in 1923. Her father owned a successful party store on Second Avenue, and the family lived in the Chicago Boulevard area. She had two brothers, Karim and John, as well as one sister, Julia. She attended a Catholic elementary school, followed by high school at Girls Catholic Central. In high school, Rosemary was always a good student who also channeled some of her energy into her sport of choice: fencing. After she graduated, she thought she might want to be a lawyer, so during 1947–49 she attended the University of Detroit School of Law—but then she took a job that changed her life. She began working at Saks Fifth Avenue and quickly discovered her passion and talent for fashion.

Her appreciation of good design in women's fashions carried over into other areas of her life as well, including an appreciation for well-designed sports cars. She owned both a Maserati MC and a Porsche. Circa 1954, there were only two Porsches in Michigan, and one of them belonged to her—and at that point, her life's path began to change again.

Rosemary Bannon is only four feet, eleven inches, so when she was sitting in the Porsche's low driver's seat, she might have been hard to see, especially while cruising down wide, multilane Woodward Avenue. And that is exactly what happened one day. She was noticed—or, more accurately, her absence was noticed—by a police detective and his partner. "There's no one driving that car!" Detective James Bannon exclaimed as they watched her Porsche drive by them. The detectives immediately began to follow her, and when they pulled her over, they were pleased to see that she had been in the driver's seat all along. Rosemary and Detective Bannon recognized each other immediately. Rosemary had seen him briefly a few weeks earlier at Saks. He had been called to the store to investigate a report of stolen merchandise.

Detective Bannon and Rosemary chatted a bit while his partner waited in the car. He told her that he would follow her home. As their discussion developed, he mentioned that he was receiving a big award later that day from the Police Department but didn't have a date to accompany him. Then he asked her if she might consider attending with him—all things considered, of course. She said, "Yes!"

Once Rosemary arrived home that day, she invited Detective Bannon inside and introduced him to her parents. The young detective hit it off immediately with Rosemary's father, Tobia, who said after he left, "This is the man Rosemary is going to marry." However, Rosemary's mother, Barbara, was horrified by Tobia's prediction and admonished him because she hoped that Rosemary would instead marry a nice Chaldean boy someday.

Nonetheless, for more than a year afterward, Rosemary and James Bannon dated before becoming engaged and marrying in 1957. Detective

Bannon came to the marriage as a widower with a young son, but both he and Rosemary hoped to have another child of their own one day. They tried to have a baby for more than nine years with no luck, and then a miracle occurred. Rosemary had visited a doctor for a checkup, but he initially misdiagnosed her pregnancy as a tumor and discussed its removal before realizing she was actually pregnant. Daughter Contessa Bannon was born several months later to James's particular delight, as he had really wanted a daughter. Ironically, Contessa would one day grow up to follow in her mother's footsteps, becoming a fashion consultant for their family-owned business, Contessa Monique. Her beloved brother, Tim, grew up to become a police officer like his father, who later became chief of police for the Detroit Police Department.

While Rosemary was married and hoping for a baby, she continued to work in fashion, rising through the ranks and developing experience at several high-fashion stores that, one by one, wooed her to them. Among her career accomplishments at Saks, she is credited with starting the idea of a personal shopper in the Oval Room there, which was very successful and which she would later develop for Hudson's. Then, in the 1960s, she was approached by Charles Himelhoch, and she went to work for him at Himelhoch's from 1962 to 1979. She recalls that one of her achievements while working there was to advocate for other women who were about to retire, many of whom had not married and had worked most of their careers for Himelhoch's. She spoke with Charles about their retirement situation. He listened and graciously wrote them generous checks to help with their retirement years.

Later, during the 1980s, Rosemary worked for Anna's Furs, located in the Penobscot Building. Once again, she was approached by a fashion store owner, Irene Miller of Claire Pearone, and she worked for her for a couple of years. After that experience, Rosemary desired a change, so she accepted a position as the executive director of the International Institute. She worked there for five years and then retired, easing back into her first love, fashion, through philanthropy and fundraising.

Rosemary quickly attracted like-minded friends in her newest endeavors to benefit worthwhile causes. One of these friends was Charlotte "Tavy" Stone, fashion writer for *The Detroit News*, who wrote about Detroit society and promoted worthwhile civic projects. Like Rosemary, Tavy was renowned for her energy and strong work ethic. With the support of Tavy and other fashionistas, Rosemary was the key organizer for one of the biggest and most successful benefits in Detroit fashion history, which was a black-tie event in 1990 at the Detroit Historical Museum to benefit the Smithsonian Archives.

Archives of American Art president Rosemary Bannon; her husband, Detroit Police Chief James Bannon; and cochair Mado Lie greet guests at the 1990 Lundi Gras black-tie dinner benefiting the Archives, Smithsonian Institution. *Photo by Bert Emanuele © Detroit Free Press/ USA TODAY NETWORK.*

Bill Blass attended, while other designers such as Mary McFadden, Gloria Vanderbilt and Xandra Rhodes sent fashions for the show.[113]

Rosemary and the Detroit Fashion Group also held benefits at Tweeneys Cafe, raising money for scholarships for students who were studying fashion and merchandising at Northwood College and the College for Creative Studies. In 1980, for these efforts and more, Rosemary was awarded Detroit Fashion Group Woman of the Year.

Tavy Stone passed away in 1985 but had already won many awards for her reporting and was inducted into the Michigan Journalism Hall of Fame in 2002. To ensure that Tavy and her work would not be forgotten, Rosemary worked with the other members of the Detroit Fashion Group to establish the Tavy Stone Fashion Library, which is now housed in the Detroit Historical Museum.[114]

Mentoring future fashionistas remains of great importance to Rosemary. She is particularly proud of having mentored Theresa Salvaggio, who became vice president of Estée Lauder and a beloved, trusted member of the Lauder family. Her advice to young people coming up in fashion is: "Be true to yourself and dress for yourself."[115]

Rosemary says she remains "fashion forward" and continues to participate locally in various worthwhile causes. In past years, she has also volunteered for Project Hope, the Red Cross and Preservation Bloomfield. She still prefers classic fashions by designers such as Valentino, but these days, her favorite place to shop for the classics is Deja Vu Upscale Designer Resale in Franklin. She says that owner Lisa Dunn has become "fashionista family" to both her and Contessa.

Rosemary's preferred reading materials are still the latest fashion magazines. However, her favorite books are the coffee table book *Louis Vuitton: A Passion for Creation* and, of course, absolutely anything about Chanel.

SUSAN SCOTT GLADWIN

BLOOMFIELD TOWNSHIP

Susan Scott Gladwin, circa 1978. *Author's collection.*

Susan Leigh Scott was a prominent fashion model in Detroit and Chicago during the 1970s, often appearing in print ads in major newspapers. She later married developer Jay Gladwin, who converted and sold as condos the formerly leased townhomes and ranch houses on Stratford Lane in Bloomfield Hills. The entire complex at the time was known as Cranbrook Manor, with the newer dwellings built circa 1970. Susan Scott Gladwin, as she became known following her marriage, was instrumental in helping her husband sell those dwellings during the early 1980s. She and Jay lived in one of the townhouses for the duration of the sales, but notably, it was Susan, in her stylish yet down-to-earth way, who seemed to help sell those dwellings quickly.

Prior to their conversion to condominiums, the newer Cranbrook Manor homes had many other prominent residents living there. Former residents and lessees included Elliot "Pete" Estes, past president of General Motors; Bob and Ruth Kemp; WWJ-TV anchor Sande Drew; architect Jack Friedman;

"Susan's Way" street sign in Bloomfield Township. *Author's collection.*

builder and book collector Toby Holtzman; automotive engineer and DMC founder John DeLorean and his wife, Cristina Ferrare; pharmaceutical company owner R.P. Scherer Jr.; Chrysler CEO Lee Iacocca; singer Eddie Kendricks of the Temptations; Matilda Citrin of Citrin Oil; business owner Jack Albright; and Chef Duglass.[116]

The ranch homes built during the early 1950s on Stratford Lane in Cranbrook Manor had notable residents as well. These included Harlan and Lola Greenwalt, whose family owned the Parsons Children's Store on Woodward Avenue, as well as Joseph and Reva Zitomer. Joseph Zitomer was the former president of Investment Realty Company and National Brands.[117]

While Susan Gladwin was helping to sell the condominiums, her husband was developing a new subdivision of stately homes off Lone Pine Road west of Telegraph Road in Bloomfield Township. In Susan's honor, he built one of the homes for her and named the street Susan's Way. Jay and Susan lived on Susan's Way for several years, which goes to show that neighborhoods, as well as people, can be quite fashionable.

PAMELA ANNE ELDRED (1948–2022)

WEST BLOOMFIELD AND FARMINGTON HILLS

"There she is, Miss America…" Those were the words that emcee Bert Parks sang as Pamela Anne Eldred was crowned Miss America in 1970 and began her "victory walk" onstage amid flashing cameras, loud applause and an American television audience of millions watching.

Pamela ("Pam") was born on April 21, 1948, in Detroit to William and Anne (née Brady) Eldred. She had two older brothers, Jerome and John, and one younger sister, Melanie. She attended Presentation School, followed by Immaculata High School, both in Detroit, after which the family moved to West Bloomfield. She graduated from the University of Detroit Jesuit High School, where she was crowned homecoming queen in 1965, which was a sign of things to come.[118]

She had always loved dance and trained in it for years, becoming a talented ballet dancer. Soon she became a principal dancer with the Detroit City Ballet, and she also trained at the American Ballet Theater in New York City. However, at one point, she suffered an injury that curtailed her career in ballet, so she returned home to Michigan and began modeling, studying at the Patricia Stevens Finishing School.

While modeling in 1968 at the Detroit Auto Show, she was recruited to participate in the Miss Detroit pageant, and later that same year, she won the title. In 1969, she entered the contest and won again. This win enabled her to compete for the Miss Michigan title, which she went on to win in 1969. From there, she competed in the Miss America pageant and was crowned Miss America 1970. In Miss America pageant history, she is known as the first ballet dancer to be crowned and the third of five Miss Michigan winners to go on to become Miss America.[119]

During her reign, Pam served two tours in Vietnam for the United Service Organizations (USO). She entertained American troops there and was later awarded two citations for "courage under fire when enemy forces prompted

Pamela Anne Eldred, Miss America 1970. *Courtesy of the Associated Press.*

evacuations during a live show."[120] Although it was a dangerous experience, Pam said afterward that her work with the USO was one of the highlights of her life.

Throughout her lifetime, Pam was also known as a special needs advocate. Her sister, Melanie, suffered from birth defects and was mentally challenged, so as Miss America, Pam became a national spokesperson for the March of Dimes. After Melanie died in 2008, Pam established the Pam Eldred Community Health Scholarship through the Miss Michigan organization, which offers scholarships to women pursuing careers that benefit the special needs community.

After her reign as Miss America, Pam returned home and earned a degree in speech and drama from Mercy College (now University of Detroit Mercy), continuing to model and perform locally. In 1976, she married Dr. Jules F. Levey, and in 1980, they moved into a new home in Farmington Hills. That same year, she gave birth to her daughter, Hilary Levey (now Hilary Levey

Friedman), who grew up to study at Harvard, Princeton and Cambridge University and become an accomplished sociologist, attorney and author of the 2020 book *Here She Is: The Complicated Reign of the Beauty Pageant in America.* Hilary married John Friedman and had two sons, with Parm becoming a doting grandmother.[121]

After Pam and her first husband divorced, Pam started her own business in cosmetology and electrolysis. She also continued to model as well as judge competitions and write for *The Oakland Press*. In 1998, Pam married lawyer Norman Robbins, and the couple divided their time between homes in West Bloomfield and Boca Raton. Norman died in 2019, and Pam passed away from kidney failure in 2022 at age seventy-four.

About her mother's life, Hilary Levey Friedman had this to say: "Pam's life ended as she lived it: on her own terms. She was sassy, strong-willed—and seriously beautiful."[122]

Chapter 8

TV NEWSCASTERS AND PERSONALITIES

Rita Bell (1925–2003)

WXYZ

For twenty-one years, beginning in 1960, Rita Bell hosted *Prize Movie* weekday mornings on Channel 7 from eight thirty to ten. She would share a classic movie with viewers, and during breaks, she would play the mystery tune of the day. Viewers could call in to guess the tune's name. The first caller to correctly name the tune would win a cash prize of $7. If the caller guessed incorrectly, $7 was added to the prize. The biggest cash prize ever given out was $4,529, on April 23, 1971, to Mrs. Shirley Gurich, who correctly named the tune "Pioneer of the Stars." After that large payout, the station gave away only products donated by local sponsors.[123]

Rita Connelly was born on June 16, 1925, in Detroit and raised there.[124] After graduating from Marygrove College with a degree in public relations, she began her career as a public relations representative for United Way.[125] She also sang with bands. However, her big break came in 1957 when the general manager of WXYZ-TV Channel 7 observed her speaking and singing at a Wrigley's corporate event. Impressed by her crowd presence, beauty, voice and pleasant personality, he asked her if she would consider working in television. She said yes, was hired and first appeared on Lou Gordon's *Midnight News Hour*. Her job, in a short segment called "Forecasts

Left to right: Rita Bell of WXYZ, Carol Duvall of WWJ-TV, Lee Murray of Station WJR and Lee Shepherd of WJBK-TV prepare for the 1965 AFTRA Ball to benefit widows and orphans of performers. © *Detroit Free Press/USA TODAY NETWORK.*

and Fashions," was to share the weather forecast as well as some fashion news. In essence, she became Detroit's and thus Michigan's first female television weather forecaster.

After two years, she was awarded her own show, which would come to be known as *Rita Bell's Prize Movie*. Her show would air more than six thousand movies during its eighteen-year run.[126] Rita, who was also an actress, had a cameo role in a 1968 episode of ABC's western television series *Big Valley*. She was also, on occasion, a national spokesperson for American Women in Radio and Television.

Rita was married to Jerome Frederick Hansen, who was a sergeant in the United States Marine Corps.[127] According to historian Gregory A. Fournier, her husband had also been a *Detroit Free Press* reporter. Following the end of Rita's TV show, the couple retired to Poway, California.

Rita Bell Connelly Hansen died at age seventy-eight on December 9, 2003, in San Diego. Her husband, Jerome, who was born in 1925, died there in 2015.[128]

DORIS BISCOE (1946–2024)

WXYZ

Doris Biscoe was a news anchor and reporter for WXYZ-TV in Southfield for more than twenty-five years. General station manager Mike Murri described his former colleague as "an incredible journalist who dominated news in Metro Detroit" and was also "strong, charming, and hardworking."[129] Born in Washington, D.C., in 1946, Doris studied communications at Howard University. At first, she worked at a radio station in Maryland. She then hosted a public affairs program in Washington, D.C., before being hired as a reporter for WXYZ, Channel 7, in 1973. At WXYZ, she began as an evening reporter before being promoted to the 6:00 p.m. news anchor. In 1995, she began anchoring the morning news.

In a 1973 *Detroit News* article, she described how she came to be hired at WXYZ: "I'd always watched Channel 7. It had the human element I liked, a relaxed atmosphere in the news. I sat down and rewrote some copy, then did a five-minute video, and they hired me."[130]

Doris Biscoe, 1995. *Courtesy of WXYZ-TV/Channel 7.*

While she was employed at WXYZ, she also hosted a weekly literacy program for children called *Learn to Read*. For her distinguished service of more than twenty-five years in broadcasting, she received the National Association of Television Arts & Sciences Silver Circle Award.[131]

Doris played the part of a newscaster in the 1987 movie *The Rosary Murders*, which was filmed in Detroit and starred Donald Sutherland. In 1998, Doris left WXYZ to start her own business, called Doris Biscoe Communications.[132]

SANDE DREW

CBS/WWJ-TV

During the 1970s and early 1980s, Sande Drew was a newscaster and anchor for CBS affiliate WWJ-TV (Channel 4) in Detroit and lived in at least two Oakland County cities during that time, including West Bloomfield. She

Sande Drew in May 1983 with friend Ray Fleming, co-owner of Birmingham's Robert Kidd Gallery. © *John Collier/USA Today Network.*

now lives in California and is a senior media consultant with her own firm, DMA Communications, which she has headed for more than twenty-four years. She also has extensive experience as a media consultant for health-related businesses.[133]

Sande is a graduate of East Texas State University and came to Metro Detroit with eight years of broadcast experience. Her skills included investigative journalism as well as on-the-air writing and producing, for which she had already earned several professional awards.[134] Before becoming a news journalist, she had been a contestant in beauty pageants such as the Maid of Cotton in 1967. She later went on to reign as Miss Dallas and was Miss Texas in the Miss America contest.

Today she lives in Sacramento, California, and has been happily married for more than twenty-five years to professional chef Karl Anders Edmond, who is originally from Stockholm, Sweden.[135]

Chapter 9

COMMUNITY LEADERS, VOLUNTEERS AND PHILANTHROPISTS

Martha Baldwin (1840–1913)

BIRMINGHAM

When visiting Birmingham, Michigan, you might notice that several venues are named Baldwin. There is Baldwin Public Library and Baldwin Park. In past years, there was also Baldwin High School, which was once an elementary school. All these places were named to honor the memory of Martha Baldwin, one of Birmingham's most productive residents, who worked in myriad ways to improve life for the people who lived there.

The sites named for her can only hint at the enormous energy she spent on behalf of her chosen community. She started out as a teacher and then became the first woman in Birmingham elected to public office, serving on and eventually becoming president of the school board. She headed drives to provide books to residents of the County Poor Farm. She was an ardent suffragist and served seven times as a representative at the National Equal Rights Convention. She was also an active member of the Women's Press Club; she worked in multiple ways to beautify the village, including advocating for maintaining Greenwood Cemetery; and she left money in her will that built Baldwin High School and created Martha Baldwin Park.[136]

The initial source of all this energy was Martha's parents, Edwin and Aurilla Baldwin. Edwin's father, Ezra, had been a pioneer, moving from Vermont to the area in 1817. His son Edwin was only fifteen when Ezra began running a successful ferry business on the Detroit River. However, Edwin was the only one of his siblings who ultimately settled and stayed in Oakland County. When Edwin was thirty-four, he married nineteen-year-old Aurilla Patrick. Edwin and Aurilla lived outside the village on a farm but were known as readers and believed that education was the route to creating a better society. Together, they would be married for fifty-two years and have only one child, Martha, and they would instill in her their own philosophies about education and creating a useful life.[137]

Martha Baldwin. *Courtesy of Baldwin Public Library.*

Martha was born in Birmingham on August 22, 1840. When she was old enough to attend school, she commuted from the family farm to the school in Birmingham. She lodged with friends there during the week, returning home to the family farm on weekends. She also attended high school in Birmingham, graduating in 1858 from what was then called the Old Academy. She studied all subjects there, excelling particularly in writing, speaking and debating. Like many young people who valued education, she had dreams of attending college and teaching school, hoping to move away to forge her own future.[138]

That same year, Martha was offered the opportunity to teach at a new school in Lexington, Michigan, which was located in Sanilac County, bordering Lake Huron. While she was ultimately successful in Lexington, growing the school's enrollment to eighteen students, she became extremely homesick. In 1859, when she was still only nineteen years old, she returned home.

Her father then moved the family to property he had purchased at what is now Maple and Chester in Birmingham. Nonetheless, Martha still had aspirations to attend college, and she was even able to attend Kalamazoo Baptist College for one year, beginning in 1860. However, the money ran out for her to attend further, as the family was experiencing financial difficulties, so once again, she returned home. At this point, Martha continued to live with her parents but also made up her mind to begin teaching school in earnest in Birmingham and its environs. Over the years, she taught in schools in Birmingham, Franklin and Detroit and even served as principal of a Detroit school that had an enrollment larger than the entire population of Birmingham. She was highly regarded for her teaching and administrative gifts but retired at age fifty-eight, in part because new rules established by the Detroit Board of Education stipulated that their educators must live in the same district where they teach. However, she was too involved with and cared too much about her hometown to acquiesce to Detroit's newest requirement.

Although Martha Baldwin never married or had children of her own, possibly because teachers were not allowed to be married when she began teaching, she had many friends and even dated several young men, including Frank Opdyke, and she taught and mentored hundreds of children over the years. Of note is one of her former students, Charles Shain, son of one of her best friends. She encouraged Charles's education, even using her own funds to help pay for his pharmacy training. He went on to have a career that became as venerated as Martha Baldwin's, and today you will find that Shain Park in the city center is named in his honor.[139]

Although Martha's most productive career years were spent as a teacher and principal, she was also active outside the classroom, striving to improve the lives of all teachers. Since there were no benefits of any kind for teachers, she helped write the Detroit Teacher's Pension Law in 1895. She also helped establish the Detroit Principal's Association as well as the Teacher's Mutual Aid Association.

Despite her myriad efforts to improve life for others, Martha Baldwin was not always liked and was even called out as being bossy or a troublemaker by people who held opposing views. Additionally, she lived during a time when it was controversial and often unacceptable for women to seek leadership roles beyond management of the home. By all accounts, she ignored these barriers and was always able to attract and organize people to get things done. Notably, Charles Shain, whom she had mentored, remained a devoted friend throughout her life. When it came to civic projects to increase the livability of Birmingham, he could be counted on to support her.

In addition to Martha Baldwin's aforementioned contributions, she was also able to complete or successfully advocate for other civic activities, including:

- Promoting the beautification of Birmingham by founding the Village Improvement Society in 1884. At that time, people still rode horses or traveled in buggies pulled by horses along unpaved roads; the work of this society was intended to help keep the roads clean and free of debris and animal waste. It also beautified the village by planting trees and flowers, especially maple trees along what is now Maple Road.[140]

- Passing an anti-spitting ordinance, getting sidewalks paved so that women wouldn't get their long skirts dirty when walking and installing wire wastebaskets on street corners.
- Improving water access and quality. This meant getting public drinking fountains installed and advocating for a waterworks system.
- Getting seating installed at streetcar stops as well as a waiting room built at the Grand Trunk Station.
- Advocating for the building and landscaping of the new train depot.
- Having a study conducted with the goal of improving the conditions at the Oakland County Jail.
- Distributing seedlings to children each year on Arbor Day to plant with their families at home.
- Driving around the city in her horse-drawn carriage and picking up litter with the assistance of many of Birmingham's children.
- Advocating successfully for the installation of the first kerosene streetlights.
- Advocating successfully for the old gravel pit on Maple Road north of Southfield Road to be turned into a park.

Perhaps the pinnacle of her contributions to Birmingham came on November 1, 1869. She held a meeting of ladies interested in forming the Ladies' Library Society of Birmingham, for which forty-eight books were purchased. This meeting led to the building of the Birmingham Public Library. However, the path to building a free library was long, at times "rancorous" and not without legal challenges.

Martha Baldwin led the initial fundraising and even contributed $2,500 of her own money toward a mortgage. The library had several different locations in its early years, but for thirty years, it was part of the Municipal Building downtown, which also housed the Police and Fire Departments, the village offices and a four-hundred-seat auditorium. As of this writing, it is a separate building, renamed for Martha Baldwin, and is undergoing extensive renovations appropriate for the needs of the twenty-first century.

When Martha Baldwin died in 1913, Birmingham was still a village; it would not incorporate as a city until 1933. The community celebrated her life by letting two hundred children out of school to carry bouquets of flowers to the Baldwin house on Maple. While the service was being held there between two and three o'clock, all local businesses were closed. Also, the Village Board officially renamed the library for Martha Baldwin. In death as in life, her contributions continued, including funds stipulated in her will for building Baldwin High School and creating two parks, as well as providing for the perpetual care of Greenwood Cemetery, where she is buried.

Matilda Dodge Wilson (1883–1967)

Rochester Hills

"To attempt great things is to expect great things. Nothing attempted, nothing gained." These famous words were spoken by Matilda Dodge Wilson, who lived a life large enough to prove them true. She is perhaps best remembered as an heiress to the Dodge fortune who became a major philanthropist, along with her second husband, Alfred G. Wilson, when she donated their estate of more than 1,400 acres of Meadow Brook Farms to Michigan State University for the building of an Oakland campus, now Oakland University. Matilda Dodge Wilson's other achievements include serving as the forty-third lieutenant governor of Michigan and building Meadow Brook Hall, her palatial home, which she and Alfred also eventually donated for public use. Meadow Brook Hall and its staff have since hosted countless public tours, holiday events, wedding receptions, conferences and educational programs; more than one hundred thousand people visit it each year.

Matilda Rausch was born in 1883 to German immigrant parents in Walkerton, Ontario, Canada. When she was only a year old, her family moved to Detroit, where she grew up and attended public school. Her mother ran a boardinghouse, while her father operated a saloon. She later graduated from Gorsline Business College in Detroit.[141]

At age nineteen, she was hired to work as a secretary for John Francis Dodge, cofounder of the Dodge Brothers Motor Company with his brother, Horace Elgin Dodge. In 1907, she married John Dodge, becoming his third wife and stepmother to John's three children from his first marriage; she would go on to have three children with him. Not long after Matilda and John married, they purchased 320 acres of a farm in the hills of Rochester, Michigan, which they began using for weekend retreats with their family and friends. They named the property Meadow Brook for the spring-fed stream that ran through the property.[142] This initial acreage would be the first of nine farms they purchased to create the contiguous Meadow Brook acreage on which Meadow Brook Hall and Oakland University would be built.

In 1916, Dodge Brothers set a record for the automotive industry when they manufactured their one hundred thousandth car only two years after they built and sold their first one.[143] For Matilda and John, as well as for Horace and his family, the significantly increasing profits meant that they were multimillionaires. Then, in 1917, after the birth of their son Daniel George Dodge, Matilda and John began planning a move from their

Portrait of Matilda Dodge Wilson by Louis Betts, 1928. *Courtesy of Meadow Brook Hall Archives.*

residence on Boston Boulevard in Detroit to a larger, grander home in Grosse Pointe—thinking that they might someday leave that home to their son. Horace Dodge and his family had already moved to Rose Terrace in Grosse Pointe, a large, impressive manor home on the shoreline of Lake St. Clair. Matilda and John wanted to build a magnificent home there as well, to "rival the most palatial structures in the world" but also to live near Horace and his family.[144]

Matilda and John hired the architectural firm of Smith Hinchman & Grylls to design their home in Grosse Pointe. Their lead architect was William Edward Kapp, who later became renowned for his interior design work on the Detroit Institute of Arts and the Guardian Building. In 1919, while the home was being built, Matilda gave birth to a daughter, Anna Margaret. During this same period, John Dodge began contributing large sums of money to Detroit charitable causes that were important to the couple, including the Salvation Army Auxiliary, the First Presbyterian Church and the Detroit Federation of Women's Clubs, among others.[145] However, during this same period, the construction of the mansion came to an abrupt halt, and it would remain unfinished for more than twenty years.[145]

In January 1920, amid the Spanish flu epidemic, which had begun in 1918, the Dodge brothers visited the National Automobile Show in New York City. Both became ill with influenza and pneumonia. On January 14, John died from pneumonia at age fifty-six at the Ritz-Carlton Hotel in New York City. His brother, Horace, still ill and devastated by John's death, died in December that same year.

Matilda Dodge immediately abandoned the construction of the Dodge mansion in Grosse Pointe. However, she faced another tragedy only a few years later. Her daughter, Anna Margaret, age four, died just before her birthday in 1924 from complications after contracting measles.

As widows, Matilda and Anna Dodge inherited millions of dollars from their husbands' estates, which included the Dodge Brothers Motor Car Company. In 1924, they decided to sell the car company to the New York investment bankers Dillon, Read and Company for $146 million, which was considered the world's largest cash transaction ever completed. Three years later, that company would sell Dodge Brothers to Chrysler Corporation; Chrysler then became one of the Big Three American automotive companies.

In June 1925, Matilda married Alfred G. Wilson, a minister's son and a lumber broker who owned Wilson Lumber Company with his brother, Donald. She had met Alfred at First Presbyterian Church in Detroit, where he served as a deacon and sang in the choir. The couple had much in common, including being the same age, sharing the same beliefs and enjoying the same types of books and music. Alfred was also civic-minded and involved in Oakland County community affairs as well as charitable activities, including the Boys' Clubs of America. He was also amenable to moving to Meadow Brook, living in the John Dodge farmhouse and expanding the farm's operations while they built a new, larger home for themselves on the property.[146]

Following their honeymoon in England, the Wilsons spent a year touring Tudor manor homes there and gathering ideas and artifacts that they wanted to incorporate into the new home they hoped to build. On their return, Matilda turned her attention to supervising the building of the grand Tudor-style manor home that would be called Meadow Brook Hall. She asked the architect, William Edward Kapp of Smith Hinchman & Grylls, to adapt some of the blueprints of rooms designed for the Grosse Pointe house for use in the new home, but ultimately, she wanted Meadow Brook Hall designed to be much grander. William Kapp visited the same English sites that held a special interest for Matilda and Alfred, copying some of the ideas as well as conducting research to accommodate their tastes and preferences.

The construction of the mansion began in 1926 and was completed for $4 million in 1929, the same year the Wilsons moved into the home. On November 19, 1929, the Wilsons held their housewarming party—less than one month after the stock market crash on October 29 and the onset of the Great Depression. Nonetheless, Matilda noted that after mailing 400 invitations, approximately 850 guests showed up despite "a terrible, slippery, stormy day," which was indicative of the strong interest people had in seeing their new palatial home.[147]

Matilda and John had no intention of living alone in the eighty-eight-thousand-square-foot Meadow Brook Hall. Her two surviving children, Frances and Daniel, whom she had with John Dodge, lived with them. Additionally, she and Alfred chose to adopt two children, Richard and Barbara, in 1930–31, and Meadow Brook Hall was where they grew up—happily, by all accounts.

Unfortunately, in 1938, Matilda's son, twenty-one-year-old Daniel Dodge, newly married and on his honeymoon, was injured in an explosion and drowned. The Wilsons brought his body home and held his funeral at Meadow Brook Hall. Distraught, Matilda closed off the wing that housed his former bedroom suite for several years.[148]

Despite this sorrowful event and a period of mourning, Frances Dodge, Matilda's firstborn daughter, went on to flourish at Meadow Brook. She

Matilda and Alfred Wilson with their children Barbara and Richard at the entrance to Meadow Brook Hall, circa 1936. *Courtesy of Meadow Brook Hall Archives.*

cultivated a love of and expertise in riding and showing horses, earning numerous awards for Meadow Brook and setting a mile record in 1940 for trotters under saddle.[149] Years later, Frances was elected to the Hall of Fame of the Trotter.

The year 1940 was auspicious in another way. Matilda was appointed as the forty-third lieutenant governor of Michigan that November, making her the first woman to serve in that position in a U.S. state. She would serve in that honorary role for only six weeks to fill a term that had not yet expired, but she felt that her appointment made a statement about women serving in government. She was quoted in *The Detroit News* on November 20, 1940, as saying, "I know that the appointment runs for only six weeks and that it, therefore, is of little importance, but I feel that it is a symbol of Gov. Dickinson's belief in the place of women in public life. It is not a compliment to me, but to the women of Michigan."

During World War II, in which the United States was officially involved from 1941 to 1945, the Wilsons were affected at home like millions of other Americans. Due to a severe shortage of fuel, Matilda closed off more than half of their house. Other items were rationed, including rubber products such as tires and even shoes.

In 1952, after their children were raised, married and had moved away, Matilda and Albert built Sunset Terrace as a retirement home for themselves on a rolling hill overlooking Meadow Brook Hall. The house had a contemporary design and, at twelve thousand square feet, was much smaller than Meadow Brook Hall. But the change in their lives got Matilda and Alfred thinking. They could do more to help the community and the state

Aerial view of Meadow Brook Hall, Rochester Hills. *Courtesy of Meadow Brook Hall Archives.*

that had been so good to them. In 1957, the Wilsons gifted $2 million and all their Meadow Brook properties to the State of Michigan. The stipulation was that the money, the land and its buildings be used to fund a university, which became Oakland University.

By all accounts, the donation thrilled the couple by what they received in return. In particular, Matilda said that some of her happiest years were spent hosting students. She came to love the university, the students and the activities centered around the school. "Education has always been an important issue for me. What I did not suspect was the depth of affection I would come to have for the students of this new university."[150]

In all, the Wilsons had occupied Meadow Brook Hall for thirty-eight years. Alfred died in 1962, and Matilda passed away from a heart attack in 1967 at age eighty-three. She was still working on behalf of Meadow Brook at the time and was in Belgium in search of new blood for her Belgian draft horses, which were being raised on the farm.[151] Afterward, Meadow Brook Hall was opened as a conference and cultural center for continuing education. It remains one of Michigan's best examples of Tudor Revival architecture and is a historical testament to the lifestyles of early twentieth-century industrialists and auto barons. In 2012, Meadow Brook Hall was designated a National Historic Landmark.

"Knowledge of the past helps people face the challenges of the future," Matilda once said.[152] She believed that the preservation of places such as Meadow Brook Hall would inspire new generations by educating them in the history of the nation.[153]

Nancy Hague

FRANKLIN

Appointed to the board at Beaumont Hospital (now Corewell Health) in Royal Oak and president for one year of all six hundred of that hospital's volunteers during her service years of 2004 to 2016, Nancy Hague became renowned as a dedicated leader who provided top-notch volunteer service. While she was president, Nancy oversaw volunteers in all parts of the hospital, including those serving in the surgical lounges, in the gift shop, at service desks and at wheelchair stations. However, her favorite area to oversee was the surgical lounges due to their importance to family members

Oakland
Echoes

Published by Oakland Hills C.C., Birmingham, MI., October 1988 Vol. 14 No. 4

WRIGHT & McCORD WIN 18 HOLE OAKLEAF

Sue Wright & Helen McCord were winners of 18 Hole Oakleaf Invitational Story on Page 4

SCHAEFER & FRIES WIN 9ERS INVITATIONAL

Mickey Schaefer & Julie Fries win 9ers Golf Invitational Story on Page 12

CORNISH & CORNISH WIN PIPER INVITATIONAL

Jeff Cornish and his brother **John,** who is a member of Mahogany Run Golf Club in St. Thomas, Virgin Islands, won the fifth flight and were overall winners of the **16th Annual Piper Golf Invitational.** The event started with a Mini-Piper practice round on July 20th with the main tournament played the following three days. The 144 teams were divided into eight flights playing a Best Ball on the South and a Chapman on the North to determine the eight teams in each flight who play the South on the final day. The Stableford point system was used for scoring and the low ten teams of each flight competed in a one day tournament on the North Course called the **Highlander.**

There were 71 teams playing the South and 16 on the North competing in the **Mini-Piper** practice rounds. Awards were presented at the contestant's stag dinner that evening. Following the tournament on Saturday, contestants and wives gathered on the veranda for cocktails and the **Piper Tatoo.** The **Scottish Highlander Band** made its appearance over the hill and piped themselves up the first fairway for a concert before the awards ceremony. Chairman, **Henry Mollicone**, Vice Chairman **Paul Babcock**, and committee members **Gerry Dietz, Art Emerson, Jack Mastin, Dick Monley** and **Pete Russell** were joined by Pro **Pat Croswell** to present the trophies to each flight winner.

Brothers Jeff & John Cornish overall Piper winners
Continued on Page 34

Left: Nancy Hague. *Courtesy of Nancy Hague.*

Right: An OHCC *Echoes* newsletter. *Courtesy of Richard Howting, OHCC Historian.*

and friends awaiting news about the surgery outcomes of their loved ones. In fact, at one point during her volunteer career before she became president, Nancy served as the chair of one of the surgical lounges.[154]

This level of volunteer leadership and responsibility might be the pinnacle achievement in anyone else's life, but for Nancy, who was also a wife and the mother, it was just one aspect of her community service. For twenty-four years, she also volunteered with her best friend, Maggie Allesee, to create the *Echoes* newsletter for Oakland Hills Country Club (OHCC). "I did the photography and layout, while Maggie did a lot of the writing," she said. "We had so much fun together. After my daughter, Laurie, gave birth to her first child, Maggie insisted she had to see the baby as soon as possible! So we had to stop working on the newsletter right then and there and made an impromptu visit. What a wonderful day that was!"

Nancy said that both she and Maggie literally started at the bottom on *The Echoes* and had to work their way up, meaning that at first, they were relegated to working on the newsletter in the basement of the country club. "But between the two of us, we didn't worry. We made sure we moved upstairs fast after that."

Nancy and Maggie first met through their husbands and their shared interest in golf. After Maggie's husband, Howard Acheson, chairman of the men's invitational golf tournament at OHCC, fell ill, Nancy's husband, Dick Hague, who was vice chairman, took over for him. She recalls that Dick enjoyed keeping score for the PGA tournaments and that OHCC always felt like a welcoming family club.

Nancy has fond memories of those days in other ways. She says that her family knew Detroit Tiger Al Kaline's family because both were members of OHCC and lived in Franklin at the same time, and when their kids were young, they went to school together. She remembers the Pinewood Derby, for which the neighborhood boys each made a racing car from a block of wood—but realistically, the dads did a lot of the work. She said that she and Al each had a son who participated in the race and that the event was great fun for everyone involved.

So how did Nancy come to live, work and volunteer in Oakland County? In 1928, Nancy was born to Mr. and Mrs. Philippe Tetrault in Madison, Wisconsin, where her father was pursuing his PhD in bacteriology (now called microbiology) at the University of Wisconsin–Madison. Once he graduated, the family moved to Lafayette, Indiana, where her father was hired to be a professor at Purdue University. Long after he passed away, she would hear from his former students who remembered him fondly.

She attended elementary school and junior high school in West Lafayette. She remembers that the junior high school was housed in a very old building and the children had to skedaddle down the fire escape during fire drills. Back in the day, the girls always wore dresses, and seeing their teacher, Miss Coulter, trying frantically to prevent her dress from flying up as she rushed down the stairs behind them amused them greatly.

Nancy graduated from West Lafayette High School at sixteen because she had done so well academically that she'd been allowed to skip two grades. Back then, she was also a big sports fan, and she remains a devoted fan of both the Detroit Lions and the Detroit Tigers.

By age nineteen, Nancy had graduated from Purdue University with a BS in microbiology, just as her father had done. Her dad even taught one of her classes—but he was tough. While in college, Nancy sang in the Purdue choir, and she worked every summer in agriculture to gain practical field experience. Being only five feet tall, she found it hard to work in the cornfields, pulling out the silk from the growing ears of corn. She couldn't easily reach the ears but somehow managed. Ironically, it was during that experience that she learned to play bridge. The students would finish half a

Left to right: Dick and Nancy Hague (*back row*) at their twenty-fifth wedding anniversary party in 1977 with their children (*front row*), Doug, Laurie and Dennis. *Courtesy of Nancy Hague.*

mile of "de-silking the corn" before sitting down to rest a spell, and during each rest period, they played bridge before moving on. "Oh, did we ever get sunburned from doing that!" she said.

Following graduation from Purdue, Nancy was hired by Parke-Davis as a researcher, which was the reason she moved to Detroit and, later, to Oakland County. At first, she stayed in the women's residence downtown across from Cass Tech, but soon she was sharing an apartment with three other young women in the Parkhurst Apartments near Indian Village.

When a friend introduced her to Dick, Nancy was smitten, and in 1952, the couple married in the Jefferson Avenue Presbyterian Church and honeymooned in the Smokies and in Gatlinburg. On returning to Michigan, they lived in a second-floor duplex on Dexter, which she says was really lovely at the time. From there, they moved and lived for a few years in Redford, where all three of their children, Dennis, Doug and Laurie, were born. For a time, her mother-in-law, Margery Hague, also lived with them; Nancy noted that she made a great babysitter whenever needed.

Nancy's husband, Dick, who had studied both business and law in Detroit, started his own business manufacturing steel bonding and rubber for lining railroad cars. He designed and built two manufacturing plants, and as his business grew increasingly successful, he and Nancy decided to build a home in Franklin, where they resided for many years. Dick's mother, Margery Hague, continued to live with them for the rest of her life, while Nancy became more and more involved with the children and their school activities until they graduated from Birmingham Groves High School and went off to college.

Dick Hague passed away in 2003, followed only a few years later by their son Dennis, who in 1993 had been one of the first heart transplant patients in Detroit. These were painful years for Nancy and the family. However, Nancy remembered her mother always telling her that things will happen and that "you do what you have to do." One year before Dick's death, they had moved to a condominium in Bloomfield's Adams Woods, and in 2004, she began her volunteer work at Beaumont Hospital, applying all her knowledge and past training wherever it was needed to help others. Her service in the surgical lounges always remained the most important to her, for by then she knew firsthand how much a caring word could mean to friends and family awaiting news about their loved ones. Now retired, Nancy enjoys knitting, crocheting and cross-stitching, and she still loves playing bridge as well as euchre, rummy, and mah-jongg with friends and family. She beams at having five grandchildren and eight great-grandchildren and treasures the family get-togethers that occur regularly, particularly at Thanksgiving and Christmas.

Dr. Indra Saini

TROY

Dr. Indra Saini fondly remembers walking with her husband, Dr. Inder Jit Saini, on the pathway along the Clinton River in the new Innovation Hills Park in Rochester Hills in 2019. They were truly enjoying their stroll through the leafy natural setting with its lovely wooden boardwalk, but when she grew tired and needed to stop and rest for a few minutes, she found there was nowhere to sit.[155] She discussed with Inder how the park could be made more comfortable for walkers, especially seniors, if benches were placed along the paths. Inder concurred. They agreed to donate benches to the park.

The couple was already listed as platinum-level donors on the park's sponsorship board for having contributed funds to the building of the children's playground, but they wanted to do even more. For this purpose, they formed the Drs. Inder Jit and Indra Saini Charitable Foundation.

Today, park benches are located throughout Innovation Hills Park, many of them donated by Indra and Inder. Since Indra and her husband wanted their visiting family members to feel a special connection to the park, they had each bench named in honor of a family member. They thought that their grandchildren, in particular, would enjoy seeing their names on a bench donated by their grandparents.

"Our gifts to the community have been repaid many times already," said Indra, "especially when we see children happy and playing, as well as people using the benches to relax. The feeling we receive in return is spiritual—like a blessing."

Indra and Inder discussed spreading even more joy in the community. They have since donated benches and funds to three other Oakland County public spaces, including the Stage Nature Center in Troy; the Sylvan Glen Park, under development just south of the Sylvan Glen Golf Course; and the Troy City Hall and Center. They are also looking to contribute benches to Boulan Park near Crooks and Wattles Roads. "The best public investment is community service," they have said, "and benches are one of the best investments for the public. These are the most needed, the most efficient, and are used by all ages, but especially by seniors."

Indra and Inder's philanthropy extends far beyond their gifts to Oakland County parks. Their recent gifts to the parks continue to make a great impact, but they have been giving to other worthy causes for more than fifty-five years. "When we see a need, we act," they said.

The Sainis built two four-story community hall buildings in India and were honored there for that major donation. Their "chain of helping others" continues in other ways as well. They also give to the Grace Centers of Hope and to the Baldwin Center. And as believers in education, they provide support for several educational scholarships, including for East Indian and American Indian students. Why American Indians? Once again, they saw the need in that category and acted. "We believe we need to show compassion for all people."

Indra and Inder are also founding members and top donors at the Bharatiya Temple on Adams Road in Troy. They live nearby and have said

Right: Dr. Indra Saini. *Courtesy of Indra Saini.*

Below: The children's playground at Innovation Hills Park. *Author's collection.*

they hope to spend the remainder of their lifetimes involved with the temple. They are ardent volunteers there, working closely with other seniors at least two days a week, which is a service they founded back in 1991. They talk and play games with other seniors, including the tabletop game carrom. They also enjoy going on outings together, including picnics and cruises.

Indra is an only child, born in 1944 to Asharfi Devi Saini and Deoki Anandan Saini in central India, where she grew up. Indra says that her parents were very well read, sharp minded and wise. Her father worked in government service, and her mother was a homemaker. Her father was transferred frequently in his job, so the family lived in several different places in central India.

For high school, Indra attended an all-girls school, although the last two years were co-ed. As she was an only child, her parents encouraged her to become a doctor so that she would always be able to support herself. Indra went on to receive her medical degree in India and became an ob-gyn and a surgeon. She also taught at a medical school there.

When Indra's parents first began to talk to her about getting married, she resisted. However, she was finally convinced when they pointed out the benefits of marriage, which included, among other things, a form of protection. Her parents had been worrying about her safety as she traveled to make doctors' home visits, which were the most common way patients received medical treatment in India at that time.

Finally, Indra agreed. She would marry—but only if she could marry another doctor. At that point, she was introduced to Inder, who had the same last name but was from a different family, and they were engaged in 1969 in Delhi. Inder was a resident in pediatric medicine at St. Joseph's Hospital in Pontiac, Michigan. He had to go back to the United States to continue his residency, but he soon returned to India to marry Indra and brought her back with him to the States to live. The couple went on to have two children, a girl and a boy, and they now also have four grandchildren.

Indra says that she has had a wonderful married life. Having been married to each other for so long, she and Inder even sometimes complete each other's sentences. However, Indra insists that they both remain open-minded. She and Inder believe they became this way by traveling the world whenever they could. Altogether, they estimate they have visited between eighty and ninety countries.

Another interest that Indra continues to enjoy is reading books about nutrition and health, as well as religion. She adds that she was not interested in cooking when she was younger, but now she enjoys it, too, because she finds it to be creative—a bit like painting, where things are combined to make something new.

She believes her biggest achievements in life are becoming a medical doctor, marrying and having children—and, through everything, remaining dedicated to and sacrificing for her family, who, in return, have made her happy and proud. "It's all connected, you see. It's not just one achievement." She said that as she reflects on her life, she feels happy, healthy and "in community."

Indra's advice to young women is for them to realize that they are "as good as the boys"—but, she says, they must also learn tolerance, as well as how to stay focused and persevere to achieve their dreams. She explained that being tolerant is particularly important because situations sometimes become difficult, even in a marriage. In order to have a successful life, knowing when to show tolerance is a necessity.

Overall, she advises all young people to respect other people, value education and explore different fields until they find exactly what it is that they want to do in life. Additionally, she advises them to listen to all sides of an issue before making any decision but also to confirm any information received.

The Saini home is a testament to what they advise others to do to achieve a worthwhile life. The walls of their home are covered with photographs of events and milestones from their lives, including time spent with their children and grandchildren. They need only to look around their home to remember what good lives they have led.

Beverly Johnson Wiggins

OAK PARK

If you ask Beverly Wiggins why she spends so many hours each week volunteering as a community service leader, she almost always answers, "To give back to the community, of course." She is dedicated to sharing with today's young people the opportunities that certain family and community members worked so hard to provide her, despite the major obstacles she had to overcome along the way. Over time, her dedication and hard work resulted in her being promoted to leadership positions in the U.S. government and major service organizations such as Kiwanis International. She has also served with and been honored by the City of Oak Park, where she has lived for many years. Notably, Beverly advanced through the government ranks to become a federal investigator for the Department of Housing and Urban Development, became the first female African American president of the Founding Club of Kiwanis International and was appointed to and served on the Oak Park City Commission for many years. But these accomplishments are just the tip of the iceberg, as she continues to lead and serve in many other capacities.[156]

Beverly was born in 1946 at Herman Kiefer Hospital in Detroit, but she was raised in Kentucky. Her parents were Mary Elizabeth Johnson and Pierce Johnson, who shared the same last name but came from different families. They separated before Beverly's birth, so figuring out how to raise Beverly fell on her mother, Elizabeth, as she preferred to be called. Elizabeth, who was from Providence, Kentucky, moved to Inkster, Michigan, to be closer to family living there but also to seek better opportunities.

To earn their keep and support Beverly, Elizabeth attended cosmetology school in Inkster and worked as a hair stylist until she began to experience

Beverly Johnson Wiggins, 2025 president of the Founding Club of Kiwanis International. *Courtesy of Barbara Wiggins.*

excessive hand pain. Elizabeth then became a cook instead. She worked at the family-owned Betty Ross Restaurant located in Palmer Park at 7 Mile Road and Woodward Avenue. That restaurant is no longer there, although a second family-owned Betty Ross Restaurant still exists at John R. and 12 Mile Roads. Years later, in the 1960s, Beverly herself worked as a dishwasher and a waitress in the family restaurant to earn the funds to put herself through college. She remembers her mother as "a very powerful, independent Black woman with long straight black hair, which reflected her one-third Native American lineage."

Beverly's mother had to work so many hours to support herself and her daughter that she worried she couldn't be home enough to properly raise Beverly. As a result, she returned Beverly to Kentucky to be raised by her Aunt Odie Mae Lawrence. Beverly understood her fragile situation and applied herself academically, graduating at age sixteen from Providence High School after being double-promoted. While in high school, she also participated in track and became a cheerleader, an activity she says put her in front of others and gave her the confidence to inspire and lead a large group.

Nonetheless, her school years in Kentucky were difficult because of racial tensions. Kentucky schools had recently become integrated, and students in various districts had to be escorted to school by national guardsmen for their protection. Beverly recalls being nervous and afraid during this period, but at the same time, she remained determined to get the best education she could manage. To Beverly, this also meant returning north after high school and seeking a college education. She explained how it had come to her that working for the U.S. government in some capacity might create a kind of "safe zone" for her as she attempted to achieve a better life. "It's true that many African Americans have sought out government work because they can see how it can make a positive difference in their own lives as well as in other people's lives," she has said. "In effect, it can be like a safety net when one is trying so hard to achieve despite constant obstacles." She said the main reason she returned to Detroit was to achieve her goal of working for the Department of Defense.

Beverly studied business at Detroit Business Institute and received her BA from that school, which has changed names over the decades but is the same institution where Henry Ford once studied. She also took classes at Wayne State University (WSU) and Wayne County Community College (WCCC) to pick up the additional credits in psychology needed for the government job she was seeking. It was while attending WCCC that she met Alonzo Wiggins, an engine tester for General Motors. They married and had one son, Brian.

After college, Beverly was hired to work for the Department of Defense. Later, she transferred to the Department of Housing and Urban Development (HUD) to continue up the career ladder as a housing counselor servicing HUD/FHA loans. After more than twenty years, she retired as a federal investigator for HUD.

Beverly received several honors for her work over the years, including an award from the U.S. secretary of HUD for rewriting the U.S. government *Housing Handbook*. She also served as president of the Southfield American Business Women's Association and was four-time president of Oak Park Kiwanis from 1994 to 1998, after which she moved to the Founding Club, which is more than one hundred years old. She then became the eighty-fourth and also the first female African American president of the Founding Club of Kiwanis International. In 2024, she became the lieutenant governor of Michigan District Division 1 and serves on that district's board. "We are involved with five different projects for Children's Hospital of Michigan, and being more than a $1 million dollar club, we are involved in coordinating the finances. In addition to handling funds for the board, we provide free books for children as well as sponsor other projects for the Detroit School System, including AKTION clubs for the mentally and physically challenged and college student Circle K clubs, of which there are ten thousand clubs total."

In 1991, City of Oak Park Mayor Gerald Naftaly and the Oak Park City Council appointed Beverly to a seat on the Oak Park City Commission. Beverly has since served under Mayor Naftaly and Mayor Rothstein, as well as three terms under Mayor McClellan. After sixteen years of service, she was appointed to serve on the Parks and Recreation Commission, and in 2010, the Oak Park City Council appointed her to be the 2010 Residential Grand Marshall for the Fourth of July parade, in which she rode in a horse-drawn carriage pulled by six Clydesdale horses. She has served in numerous other capacities, including as commission secretary. In that position, her duties included overseeing the Oak Park Fruit Market and Forgotten Harvest Food Truck, senior group classes and recreational programs and numerous activities involving the city's children. "What a life it has been!" she has said.

Additionally, Beverly is also on the board of the Empowerment Zone Coalition, a drug prevention organization funded by the City of Detroit. "It's a joy to belong to something that is making a real difference in young people's lives!" she has said.

Beverly is also very entrepreneurial and started an Amway business in 1998 that earned the income to send her son, Brian, through college. If she seems "all work and no play," don't worry; Beverly occasionally has free time for hobbies, which include sewing, cooking and carpentry.

MIA MATERKA

BLOOMFIELD HILLS

If a polymath is a person of wide-ranging knowledge who achieves excellence in many different areas, then this term perfectly describes Mia Materka. She has been an outstanding student and lover of literature, a software developer, a writer and editor of technical publications, a marketing professional, a wife to a prominent physician—and since getting married, a busy volunteer, fundraiser and philanthropist for multiple worthy causes with the goal of improving the lives of others. She is also devoutly Catholic.[157]

Left to right: Dr. Stan Materka, Mia Materka, TV host Regis Philbin and Brother Francis Boylan of the Congregation of the Holy Cross at a Good Samaritans benefit in 2015. *Courtesy of Mia Materka.*

Mia was born in Manila, the Philippines, to Cecilio (named after Saint Cecilia) and Concessa (named after Saint Concessa). She has one sister and one brother, who live in Florida. Her father was half French and half Spanish, while her great-grandmother was from France. Her family immigrated to the United States in 1974, at first living in New York but later settling in Boca Raton, Florida, because they found the New York climate to be too cold and harsh. Mia attended St. Joan of Arc Catholic School in Boca Raton and later graduated with honors from Cardinal Gibbons High School in Fort Lauderdale.

While attending college at Florida Atlantic University, Mia majored in and received her BA in European literature, graduating with honors. She has noted that her interest in literature and storytelling extends to her ancestors who have inspired her, particularly to her paternal grandfather, who is credited with founding the movie industry in the Philippines. To honor his memory and contributions to filmmaking, a stamp was issued in his name in 2019.

"I stand on the strong shoulders of those who came before me," she has said. "We are known to be focused, disciplined and resilient." She has said that the stereotype of the demure Asian woman does not apply to the women in her family, noting that there has been a strong matriarchal line all along that became particularly strong during World War II. She has noticed that many of her relatives, with the exception of a cousin who is a retired judge, have excelled in math and science careers. She cites as an example her aunt Aurelia Romero, who was a biochemist at Cornell University.

Following her own graduation from college, Mia was hired by IBM as a software developer. Back then, computers were still relatively new, and employees who understood how computers worked and could explain that information to customers were greatly needed. Mia wrote many of IBM's manuals and books, which meant translating, writing and editing technical information for new users. Significant projects she worked on also included the early development of the Internet, the development of voice recognition technology and the remediation of systems for Y2K compliance.

To progress in the computer industry, which was quickly expanding internationally, Mia moved to Michigan to earn an MS in international administration at Central Michigan University's satellite campus in Metro Detroit. From there, she moved into marketing. Metro Detroit is also where she met her future husband, Dr. Stan Materka, an attending physician at Detroit Receiving Hospital. A mutual friend introduced her to him, while Mia has said that she in turn introduced Stan to restaurants and dining, an

Mia Materka (*far right*) with guests, including Missionary Sisters of Charity, 2023. *Courtesy of Mia Materka.*

area with which he was unfamiliar due to his heavy work schedule. She has said that although she can be perceived as quiet at times, Stan told her that what he most liked about her was that she is a formidable person. He wanted to be with a woman who was strong and independent and could stand on her own, especially when he could not be around all the time.

Once Mia and Stan married, her own life changed to better accommodate Stan's and her own busy schedules. Now retired, she dedicates a good deal of her time to giving back to the community. She has been extremely active in fundraising for Friends of Preservation Bloomfield, helping to raise more than $1 million and serving as that organization's first and, as of this writing, only president of Asian descent. In 2018, she was honored with the Preservationist of the Year Award for her efforts that truly went above and beyond. Mia is also past president of the Altar Guild at St. Hugo's Church in Bloomfield Hills and past president of the Good Samaritans. For several years, she has been the membership chair for the Ladies of Charity of St. Vincent de Paul of Oakland County, where she has been involved in numerous social and fundraising activities with her dear friends

Denny Dinan-Panico and Carol Shaya, who have also been highly active in fundraising and providing volunteer services to the church community. For the Ladies of Charity members, in 2023, Mia organized a special and inspiring visit of nuns from the Missionary Sisters of Charity, along with a movie presentation about the life of Mother Teresa, both of which were extremely well received. In 2025, Mia became president of the Ladies of Charity of St. Vincent de Paul of Oakland County.

When Mia is not giving back to the community, she enjoys working out in her home's gym. She also enjoys music, having studied piano her whole life and performed in recitals. Her favorite composers have always been Chopin, Bach and Rachmaninoff. Here, once again, she stands on strong shoulders, for her father also played the piano naturally and instinctively, while both her mother and her niece were opera singers.

IN HER OWN WORDS

Researching Lillian Drake Avery

By Barbara L. Frye

Barbara L. Frye. *Courtesy of Barbara Frye.*

When you retire from your workaday job, you are free to reinvent yourself. You are free to follow your bliss and really utilize your talents. Volunteering at Oakland County Pioneer and Historical Society has given me that freedom. Doing historical and genealogical research for patrons has been particularly fulfilling. Portraying one of my research subjects, Lillian Drake Avery, for an Oak Hill Cemetery Walk in Pontiac and other events has been a special joy.

In researching Mrs. Avery's life to better represent her, I was struck by the similarities in our lives. Her father was an amateur photographer, my father chose photography as his profession and both men had a darkroom in their home. Lillian was an artist, as am I. Lillian was very interested in history; I have an interest there as well. Lillian was a charter member of her Daughters of the American Revolution chapter in 1900; I am a charter member of my DAR chapter. Lillian Drake Avery was the secretary of the Oakland County Pioneer and Historical Society for close to twenty years; I am currently the board secretary of that same society. But curious similarities aside, I needed more background information to bring this amazing lady to life.

Lillian Drake Avery. *Courtesy of Oakland County Pioneer & Historical Society.*

So who was Lillian Drake Avery? Lillian Drake was born on a farm in Farmington, Michigan, on November 22, 1822. She attended primary school and graduated from Chelsea High School in 1875. Several times during her education, she was asked to serve as a teacher to younger students. In fact, after graduation, she taught primary school in Farmington for three years. One of her schoolmates was Aaron B. Avery, who continued his studies to become a doctor, practicing first in Farmington. Before he left for Ann Arbor, Aaron asked Lillian to be his wife, and they were married on October 22, 1879. The couple relocated to Pontiac in November 1885, raising two daughters there.

As mentioned, Mrs. Avery served as secretary of the Oakland County Pioneer Society for many years. (She is the reason we have the splendid scrapbook recording the events of the 1916 Oakland County Centenary and other scrapbooks.) From 1886 to 1894, she was the director of the Ladies' Library Association and a member of the Chautauqua Circle and the Round Table Club. In 1892, she organized and was the first president of the Woman's Literary Club. Additionally, in 1900, she was an organizing member of the General Richardson Chapter of the Daughters of the American Revolution, and she served as its first vice regent. She also served as regent, historian and registrar of her chapter. On top of all this, she was active in the Norton Avenue Hospital Guild, the Girls' Protective League, the Romans' Auxiliary of the American Legion—and perhaps more. Lillian also collected the stories and recorded the history of Oakland County and was "regarded as probably the best-versed individual in the state on the early history of this section" (from her obituary).

Left to right: Marion Eliza L. TenEyck, Marcia Marie Richardson, Mabel Thorpe, Lillian Drake Avery and Ada Louise Leggett Smith. *From the Pioneer Album—Archives, Oakland County History Center. Courtesy of Oakland County Pioneer & Historical Society.*

Lillian Drake Avery was a teacher, librarian, historian, activist, mother and doctor's wife. She was a member of the Michigan Pioneer and Historical Society and was the editor of *An Account of Oakland County*, volume 3 of *Historic Michigan: Land of the Great Lakes*, published in honor of the society's fiftieth anniversary. She was also the moving force behind discovering and recording the histories of the Revolutionary War veterans in our area. In my Patriot Project, I have tried to expand on Mrs. Avery's work and that of her chapter members to tell the stories of the veterans she found and to find others with today's resources. Her scrapbooks and records have proved a valuable resource for research to this day.

In researching the records she left to the society, I discovered a curious photograph. It was a group portrait of five women in colonial attire dated 1900. The photo seemed a little late for that finery. Research proved the photograph is of the first Colonial Ball Reception Committee of the General Richardson Chapter of the NSDAR, an event held as an annual fundraiser until at least 1909. Lillian Drake Avery, vice regent, is the fourth lady from the left.

Lillian Drake Avery led a fascinating and fulfilling life, from being a farm girl in Farmington to becoming an educated and active woman in a thriving community, and she left us stories and historical accounts that color an era. In 1916, on Woman's Day, Mrs. Avery received the Insignia of Good Citizenship from the Oakland County Equal Suffrage Association. Viewing her watercolors and reading her accounts gave me the background I needed to bring this exciting woman to life for a community curious about "the little woman."[158] Far from drab and retiring, this librarian had some surprises for us. It was a pleasure researching her many accomplishments and sharing them with you, gentle reader.

Chapter 10
SINGERS AND QUEENS OF SONG

Aretha Franklin (1942–2018)

BLOOMFIELD HILLS

The Queen of Soul, Aretha Franklin, needs little introduction, so vast has been the reach of her singing and songwriting talents. "Respect," "Chain of Fools" "I Say a Little Prayer," "Do Right Woman—Do Right Man," "Who's Zoomin' Who?" "Freeway of Love" and "I Never Loved a Man (the Way I Love You)" are just a few of her many hit songs that are now modern classics. During her lifetime, she sold more than seventy-five million records worldwide and was the first female performer to be inducted into the Rock and Roll Hall of Fame.[159] In addition, in 2005, she was presented with the Presidential Medal of Freedom, and over the span of her career, she received eighteen Grammy Awards. Twice, *Rolling Stone* magazine named her the greatest singer of all time.

Aretha Franklin's powerful singing voice emerged when she was a young girl singing in the gospel choir of New Bethel Baptist Church in Detroit, where her father, Reverend C.L. Franklin, was the minister. As the years passed and her music career grew increasingly successful after she signed with Atlantic Records in 1966, she bought and lived in homes in several places, including Detroit and Bloomfield Hills. Her homes at various times in Bloomfield were located off Echo Road, on County Club Drive and in the Turtle Creek gated community.

Aretha Franklin. *Photo by Norman Parkinson. Courtesy of the Burton Historical Collection, E. Azalia Hackley Collection, Detroit Public Library.*

"I'm the lady next door when I'm not on stage," Aretha Franklin once said about herself.[160] Despite being world-famous, she was perceived locally as being family-oriented and down-to-earth when she wasn't performing. "I talked to her when she came into our deli, and I always thought, 'What a nice lady she is,'" said Joseph, a member of the family that has owned and operated Bloomfield Deli on Long Lake Road since 1992. Aretha Franklin was also known for her volunteer work. She could be found volunteering hands-on, just like most anyone else, at telethons and other worthy events that benefited various charities and causes around Metro Detroit. These included fundraisers for Easter Seals and the Detroit Institute of Arts, as well as a campaign against driving under the influence of drugs or alcohol. Aretha once said about volunteering in one's own community: "Being the Queen is not all about singing, and being a diva is not all about singing. It has much to do with your service to people. And your social contributions to your community and your civic contributions as well."[161]

Aretha Louise Franklin was born the fourth of five children on March 25, 1942, in Memphis, Tennessee, to Clarence LaVaughn (C.L.) Franklin and Barbara Siggers Franklin. C.L. Franklin was a Baptist minister, while Barbara was a gospel singer and pianist.

When Aretha was only six years old, her parents separated, and her mother left Aretha in the care of her father. Only four years later, her mother died from a heart attack. About that time, Reverend Franklin relocated to Detroit to pursue preaching opportunities, eventually becoming the minister at New Bethel Baptist Church, where he was known for his "Million Dollar Voice" and brilliant sermons, which were recorded with Chess Records.[162] The apple did not fall far from the tree.

Aretha, who was mostly self-taught as a musician, began singing in the New Bethel Baptist Church choir as well as playing the piano there. Soon she was singing in front of the entire congregation. The power of her voice and her gifts as a pianist led members of her congregation to label her a child prodigy. Then, in 1956, at age fourteen, she recorded some of her earliest tracks at church, which were released as the album *Songs of Faith* on a small music label. She also began touring with her father's traveling revival show around the country, where she met and was inspired by other great singers, including Mahalia Jackson, Sam Cooke and Lou Rawls.[163] Mahalia Jackson became a lifelong mentor and confidante, while Sam Cooke and Lou Rawls, who had gospel singing backgrounds, gave Aretha advice that she could use as she transitioned to singing commercially.

Four years later, with her father's blessing, Aretha traveled to New York, where she signed with Columbia Records. She released her first album, *Aretha*, in 1961 and achieved some initial success with Columbia, especially when her first single, "Today I Sing the Blues," climbed to no. 10 on the R&B charts. However, her distinctive voice and style had not yet emerged, as the label was still experimenting and had her mingling gospel and blues along with cabaret and Broadway show–type music. It wasn't until music producer Jerry Wexler and Aretha's new husband and manager, Ted White, convinced her to move to Atlantic Records in 1966 that she hit the bull's-eye musically.[164]

The late 1960s were years of great change and tumult, despair and hope, and Aretha's beautiful, powerful voice fit the mood. Her first single produced by Jerry Wexler was "I Never Loved a Man (the Way I Love You)." It was recorded in a one-day session at Rick Hall's FAME Recording Studios in Muscle Shoals, Alabama, marking Aretha's emergence as "a prodigious talent but [also]…the start of a new era of fresh, forthright soul music."[165] The single became a national top 10 hit.[166]

Then, when Aretha was still only twenty-five years old, she recorded Otis Redding's "Respect" as the first song for her album *I Never Loved a Man (the Way I Love You)*. In taking that song to a new level, she became known as Lady Soul. "Respect" was released as a single and reached no. 1 on both the R&B and pop charts; Aretha won her first two Grammy Awards for it.[167]

Aretha was clearly on her way. She continued to experiment with records and albums such as *Gifted and Black*, *Spirit in the Dark* and what is called her tour de force, *Amazing Grace*. She also performed successfully before live audiences at the Apollo Theatre and the Fillmore West.

A new string of no. 1 single hits followed, including "Baby I Love You," "Chain of Fools," "Think," "I Say a Little Prayer," "Since You've Been Gone" and "(You Make Me Feel Like) A Natural Woman." From that point on, she was known as the Queen of Soul and also as a symbol of Black

Aretha Franklin in 1968. *Courtesy of Wikimedia Commons.*

empowerment. In 1968, she performed at the funeral of Dr. Martin Luther King Jr. That same year, she was invited to sing the national anthem at the beginning of the Democratic National Convention.[168]

While her hits kept coming, Aretha suffered a personal setback in 1969 when she and Ted White divorced. However, by 1972, she was back and at the top of her game when she returned to her gospel roots after Mahalia Jackson's death. That was the period in which she recorded the album *Amazing Grace*. That album sold more than two million copies and was considered the best-selling gospel album ever at the time.

Aretha's success continued during the remainder of the 1970s. She expanded her repertoire into pop and rock, and the single "Ain't Nothing Like the Real Thing" won her her eighth Grammy Award. Then a period of ups and downs began. By 1975, disco music had become the rage, and new singers were emerging, including Donna Summer and Chaka Khan. For the first time, Aretha's music was becoming less popular. However, she still experienced special moments, like when she was invited in 1977 to perform at the inauguration of President Jimmy Carter. "Music changes, and I'm gonna change right along with it," she once said.[169] She also found love again and, in 1978, married actor Glynn Turman.

However, the year 1979 was a return to sorrow for Aretha. Her beloved father, Reverend C.L. Franklin, was shot during a burglary attempt at his home, which left him in a coma. Aretha moved back to Detroit to help care for him. Then, due to a string of chart failures that same year, Aretha's relationship with Atlantic Records was terminated. On top of this, she received a huge bill from the Internal Revenue Service.

Aretha's cameo appearance in the 1980 movie *The Blues Brothers* and her performance of "Think" with comedians John Belushi and Dan Aykroyd soon revived her popularity with R&B lovers as well as her income. In addition, with the help of singer-songwriter Luther Vandross, in 1982, she was signed to Arista, and with that came more recording successes. In 1982, her song "Jump to It" became a dance hit. However, in 1984, Aretha suffered another downturn. She and Glynn Turman divorced, and her father died.

Aretha was notably resilient. By this stage in her life, she also had four sons to look after, which helped her to continue moving forward. Three of her sons would later become involved, in different ways, in the music industry themselves. Her son Edward became a gospel singer; her son Teddy was a backup guitarist for his mother's band and also performed with Al Green and Joe Cocker; and her youngest son, Kecalf, became a gospel rapper who sang with his mother at Radio City Music Hall.[170]

By 1985, Aretha was at the top of the charts again with her album *Who's Zoomin' Who?* The single "Freeway to Love" as well as her collaboration with the rock band the Eurythmics contributed to the album's success, making it her best-selling album ever. Then her 1986 album, *Aretha*, eventually went gold, and in 1987, Aretha Franklin became the first female artist inducted into the Rock and Roll Hall of Fame. She also received an honorary doctorate from the University of Detroit.[171]

According to author and photographer Linda Solomon in her 2019 book *The Queen Next Door*, Aretha developed a fear of flying in the 1980s. Therefore, to record with her, other singers and musicians, including music legends Keith Richards and Ronnie Wood of the Rolling Stones, had to come to Detroit to record. And so they did. Richards and Wood recorded "Jumpin' Jack Flash" with her, which became the title song of the movie of the same name.

If all these achievements were not enough, her album *One Lord, One Faith, One Baptism*, which was released in 1987, won her yet another Grammy for Best Soul Gospel Performance. "For years, people have been asking me to record gospel again," Aretha said, "so I decided it was time. These are the songs I loved as a child singing in the choir."[172]

In 1993, Aretha Franklin was invited to sing at the inauguration of Bill Clinton. Within the next year, she received a Kennedy Center Honor, as well as a Grammy Lifetime Achievement Award.

Three other outstanding moments for Aretha took place as the twentieth century was drawing to a close. Having studied opera for twenty years, Aretha sang Puccini's "Nessun dorma" to rave reviews in 1998, standing in for Luciano Pavarotti, who was too ill to sing and receive his own lifetime achievement award at the Grammy Awards that year. Then, taking on her former role in the movie *Blues Brothers 2000*, she hit gold once more with the song "A Rose Is Still a Rose," which was released as the lead single in 1998 for her album of the same name. In 1999, she was awarded a National Medal of Arts from the National Endowment for the Arts, which President Bill Clinton presented to her in Washington, D.C.

The new millennium saw her moving full steam ahead with no clear intentions of slowing down. After she recorded her last album, *So Damn Happy*, with Arista Records in 2003, she formed her own record company, called Aretha. In 2005, she received the Presidential Medal of Freedom. In 2008, she received her eighteenth Grammy Award, for "Never Gonna Break My Faith."

The accolades kept coming. Three years later, she returned to her label and recorded her first album there: *A Woman Falling Out of Love*. Several years after that, she recorded *Aretha Franklin Sings the Great Diva Classics*, which scored high on both the R&B and pop charts. She would never really retire fully, and in 2017, at age seventy-four, she even announced she was working with Stevie Wonder on a new album. However, later that same year, she became increasingly ill, and she passed away from pancreatic cancer in her Detroit home on August 12, 2018. As Aretha had always hoped, Oscar-winner Jennifer Hudson portrayed her in a musical biopic, titled *Respect*. The film, which was released in 2021, won several awards and was dedicated to Aretha Franklin.[189]

"Being a singer is a natural gift," Aretha once said. "It means I'm using to the highest degree possible the gift that God gave me to use. I'm happy with that."[173]

Madonna

Rochester Hills

When aspiring American actors, singers, dancers or other performers want to "make it big," they usually move to either New York City or Los Angeles. The odds remain stacked against them: less than 1 percent among millions ever achieve stardom.[174] Nonetheless, Rochester Hills' own Madonna Louise Ciccone took the leap at age twenty, dropping out of the University of Michigan in 1978 to move to New York City. With enormous talent, drive, perseverance, moxie and a bit of luck, she gave music stardom her best shot and beat the odds.

Madonna, the Queen of Pop, is the first entertainer to gross more than $1 billion in concert tours and is the world's best-selling female recording artist of all time. In 2008, she was inducted into the Rock and Roll Hall of Fame. She has received seven Grammy Awards; had fifty-eight hit songs; won a

Madonna in 2023. *Photo by Raph_Ph. Courtesy of Wikimedia Commons.*

Golden Globe Award for Best Actress, for the movie *Evita*; and received more than four hundred awards and honors in other categories, including honorary Brazilian citizenship for her 2024 Celebration Tour in Rio de Janeiro.

After more than forty years in the entertainment business, she remains as provocative as when she had her first hit record, continuing to reinvent herself and her acts to provide entertainment that attracts and pleases her audiences worldwide. "I do my best! I do my best!" she shouted in 2024 to a crowd of thousands in San Francisco after nearly two hours of performing in her epic Celebration Tour there. That tour was a retrospective that summarized her life's creative achievements and included famous past hits such as "Vogue," "La Isla Bonita," "Express Yourself," "Into the Groove," "Holiday," "Like a Virgin," "Material Girl," "Blonde Ambition," "Everybody," "Open Your Heart," "Like a Prayer," "Justify My Love," "Nothing Really Matters," "Don't Cry for Me Argentina" and "Celebration," among others.[175]

Usually associated with her concert performances are shock elements that, in the past, have included French kissing Britney Spears on stage, singing in the midst of scantily clad dancers or titillating her audience in some other suggestive way. Don't think that these elements weren't carefully planned, however. She has been incorporating them for decades, which makes her audiences love or loathe her—but she never bores them.[176] When she left Metro Detroit in 1978, she said, "I'm gonna be someone," and she meant it.

Madonna Louise Ciccone was born on August 16, 1958, in Bay City, Michigan, to Silvio Anthony "Tony" Ciccone and Madonna Louise (née Fortin), a Catholic couple. Tony was an optics engineer for military projects and worked for Chrysler Defense and, later, General Dynamics Land Systems. Madonna's mother was of French Canadian descent and was a homemaker. In all, there were five other children in addition to Madonna. At first, the children were raised in a modest home in the Herrington Hills neighborhood of Pontiac; later, the family moved to a larger home on Oklahoma Street in Rochester Hills (formerly Avon Township).

In 1963, when Madonna was a quiet, shy five-year-old, her mother died from breast cancer, which she has always said traumatized her. Then, only three years later, Tony married the family's housekeeper and nanny, Joan Gustafson; Joan would give birth to two children with Tony. Madonna resented her father's remarriage, feeling betrayed and alone, and she began rebelling against him, which caused a strain in their relationship for many years. In a 1991 interview with *Rolling Stone*, she said her attitude was: "Okay, I don't have a mother to love me. I'm going to make the world love me!"[177]

Madonna and her siblings also resented the strict regimen their stepmother had them follow, which Madonna said made her feel for years like she was Cinderella. Nonetheless, Madonna developed discipline, which helped her channel her sadness into work. And being one of six children, she also learned to become an extrovert. "If I wanted my father's attention, I would get on a table and tap dance and lift my dress—and guess what—he'd pay attention to me."[178]

Madonna attended St. Frederick and St. Andrew Catholic Elementary Schools, West Middle School and, later, Rochester Adams High School, graduating from Rochester Adams with straight A's. Despite always studying hard and getting good grades, she acted up in unusual ways all through her school years, such as hanging upside down on the monkey bars and exposing her underwear in elementary school or not shaving her underarms and legs in high school. Nonetheless, she was athletic and made the high school cheerleading squad. In high school, she also started the Thespians Club.[195]

To help develop her interests, Tony had Madonna take piano lessons, but she said that she preferred to study ballet, which she later did with Christopher Flynn in Rochester. Flynn recognized Madonna's talent and encouraged her to seek a career in dance. Madonna likewise encouraged her brother, Christopher, to study dance at the same school, which he did, and in later years he worked closely with Madonna as a dancer and as the art director for her Blond Ambition World Tour.[179]

When Madonna was still in high school, she began visiting underground gay dance clubs in Detroit. She had heard that they were places of great theatricality and freedom, and she found that to be true. She would continue visiting such clubs and supporting the rights of the LGBT community throughout her career.

In 1976, when she graduated from high school, she received a four-year dance scholarship to the University of Michigan. However, in 1978, in part due to the encouragement of Christopher Flynn, who was then teaching at the university, she dropped out and headed to New York City.

Her initial experiences in New York were tough. She arrived with only thirty-five dollars left after paying her travel expenses. Poor and hungry, she crashed on couches and was robbed several times in her early years there.

She took low-paying jobs, like being an artist's model, but also began to get hired as a backup vocalist and a dancer. In addition, she started attending Danceteria, a key dance club in the city. One evening, she approached the DJ, Mark Kamins, with a cassette demo she had made of her singing "Everybody" and asked him to play it, which he did. Kamins also happened to be a talent scout for Sire Records. He so liked what he heard that he connected her to Sire president Seymour Stein, who paid Madonna $15,000 for two singles. Madonna was on her way.[180]

In 1983, Sire produced her first album, called *Madonna*, which she dedicated to her father. It sold more than ten million copies and was listed on the Billboard 200 for 168 weeks. The timing of her album's release was fortuitous because there was no other music out like it. Her sound was not only unique but also coincided with the start of MTV, which played videos that combined music, song and dance—all the talents that Madonna first began developing back in Oakland County, Michigan.

After that, Madonna would go on to success after success and expand her repertoire to acting in films, including *Dick Tracy*, *Evita* and *A League of Their Own*; writing children's books, such as *The English Roses*; and creating her own entertainment company called Maverick, which included Maverick Records and divisions for merchandising, television, film and more. Over the years, she would also fall in love, marry and divorce twice and give birth to and adopt children. In 2006, she founded the Raising Malawi charity after a humanitarian visit to Africa and adopted four Malawian children who, on occasion, join her in performing. Her future plans include creating her own biopic.

Madonna singing during her Rebel Heart Tour in Stockholm, 2015. *Photo by chrisweger. Courtesy of Wikimedia Commons.*

"I hope you're proud of me, Detroit!" Madonna said to a crowd of thirteen thousand when she returned to Metro Detroit in 2024 to perform in her Celebration Tour concert at

Little Caesars Arena. "I care what you think, and I want you to be proud of me."[181] Her ninety-two-year-old father, Tony, who has Parkinson's disease, was in the audience. She honored him with a tribute that was emotional and heartfelt. After four decades of performing, it was clear that nothing can last forever, including Madonna, but it was really nice to have her back in town for a while to witness her amazing success.[182]

Chapter 11

STAGE AND SCREEN ACTRESSES

Patricia Ellis (1918–1970)

BIRMINGHAM

Patricia Ellis was an American film actress and singer who came to prominence in films from 1932 to 1939. Her singing career continued until 1941. She was born Patricia Gene O'Brian in Birmingham on May 20, 1918, the oldest of four children. Her parents were Eugene Gladstone O'Brien, an insurance salesman, and Florence (née Calkins) O'Brien. They married on April 16, 1917, and divorced twelve years later.[183]

Patricia and her siblings lived with their father during the school year while staying with their mother during the summer months. Then Patricia's mother married Alexander Leftwich, a producer of musical shows, after which Patricia became known as Patricia Leftwich but kept Patricia Ellis as her stage name. At some point, she moved to New York to live with her mother and stepfather.

Her memories of childhood activities from then on were of singing, dancing and studying French and German. She attended Brantwood School in Bronxville, New York, and Gardner School for Girls in New York City. She learned about acting by watching her stepfather audition actresses and then understudying them. After leaving school, Patricia began her stage career while also taking classes to learn about movie studios and their facilities.

Movie poster featuring Patricia Ellis, 1938. *Courtesy of Wikimedia Commons.*

When Patricia was still in her teens and acting in a stage play in New York, she did a screen test for Warner Brothers and sent it to the studio. The studio liked what it saw and signed her to act in movies, and she soon left for Hollywood. Along with Ginger Rogers, Gloria Stuart and other young actresses, she was named a WAMPUS Baby Star of 1932, an honor that meant she was on the cusp of stardom. At first, she was given only small parts, but then she worked her way up to second leads and was soon averaging seven films a year. Her first credited role came in 1933 in the film *The King's Vacation*, starring George Arliss and Marjorie Gateson. Although she worked steadily, she appeared mostly in lower-budget B movies, which frustrated her. However, later in 1933, she costarred with James Cagney in *Picture Snatcher.* In 1936, she costarred again, this time with Bela Lugosi in

Postal Inspector. Some of the other films she appeared in were *The Gaity Girls*, *Fugitive at Large* and *Here Comes the Groom*, costarring Jack Haley.[184]

Patricia felt she had peaked by 1939 and gave up acting, returning to singing on Broadway in the musical hit *Louisiana Purchase*, as well as singing in the musical revue *Hollywood Stars on Parade*. She also sang in accompaniment with orchestras through 1941. On July 12, 1942, Patricia married George T. O'Malley, who became president of Protection Securities Systems, and the couple moved permanently to Kansas City. They had one daughter. On March 26, 1970, at age fifty-one, Patricia passed away from cancer.

Elaine Stritch (1925–2014)

Birmingham

Elaine Stritch in 1973. *Photo by Allen Warren. Courtesy of Wikimedia Commons.*

Elaine Stritch is a Broadway legend. She acted on stage for more than fifty years and, to a lesser extent, on television, becoming known for her raspy voice and wry comic timing.[185] The critic Rex Reed once wrote about her: "Elaine Stritch can still stop you in your tracks with a meaningless, drop-dead one-liner."[186] During her lifetime, she won four Emmy Awards, a Tony Award and a Grammy. In 1995, she was inducted into the American Theater Hall of Fame.[187]

Elaine was the third and last daughter born on February 2, 1925, in Detroit to George Joseph Stritch, a rubber company executive, and his wife, Mildred (née Jobe), a homemaker. The family later moved to Birmingham.

As a young woman, she dreamed of having a glamorous life, so she moved in 1944 to New York City to seek her fortune. She trained alongside actors such as Marlon Brando at the Dramatic Workshop of the New School for Social Research. Afterward, she worked constantly in regional theater and off Broadway before making her Broadway debut in the comedy *Loco* in 1946.

From then on, she never looked back, becoming one of the most famous actresses to ever act on Broadway. She died at her home in Birmingham, Michigan, on July 17, 2014.

KRISTEN BELL

HUNTINGTON WOODS

Kristen Bell in 2013 at the *Frozen* Premiere, Hollywood. *Courtesy of Wikimedia Commons.*

Metro-Goldwyn-Mayer (MGM) once claimed it had "more stars than there are in heaven," and Oakland County might just be an incubator for them. Per research by TicketSource, Michigan is eighth overall in the nation for having produced "stars," with a total so far of 4,001.[188] Kristen Bell is one of them. In addition to her dramatic skills, she is known for her beautiful singing voice. She sang the part of Princess Anna in the highly successful 2013 Disney film *Frozen* and, later, in *Frozen 2* (2019). Kristen is also famous for her lead role in the television series *Veronica Mars*, which aired from 2004 to 2007. She later reprised that role in two spinoff films distributed by Warner Bros. She has acted in countless other productions and has received Golden Globe nominations for her lead roles in the NBC comedy series *The Good Place* and the 2024 Netflix romantic comedy series *Nobody Wants This*.

Kristen Anne Bell was born and grew up in Huntington Woods. Her father was a television news director, and her mother was a nurse. She was still a baby when her parents divorced, but both her parents remarried and had more children, resulting in her having twelve step- and half-siblings. Young Kristen showed an early interest in acting, and her mother enrolled her in private acting lessons and also signed her with an agent when she was twelve. She went on to appear in local television commercials and in newspaper ads for Detroit retailers.

Kristen attended public schools in Berkley and, later, Shrine Catholic High School in Royal Oak. At Shrine, she shone as an actress in school plays. She won the lead role of Dorothy in *The Wizard of Oz* and acted in other plays, including *Fiddler on the Roof* and *Li'l Abner*.

In 1998, Kristen graduated from Shrine and moved to New York City to attend the Tisch School of the Arts at New York University. She left the university just short of graduating in 2001 to act in the Broadway musical version of *The Adventures of Tom Sawyer*. That year, she had her first credited film debut in the movie *Pootie Tang*. Then, in 2002, she moved to Los Angeles, where she began to appear in a host of television programs. Her first acclaimed role came in 2004 when she starred in the Lifetime television film *Gracie's Role*. She has been acting ever since. In 2013, she married actor Dax Shepard, who grew up in Milford and Walled Lake, and in 2019, she received a star on the Hollywood Walk of Fame.[189]

SELMA BLAIR

SOUTHFIELD

Metro Detroit born and bred Selma Blair is an actress who became famous for her roles in the movies *Legally Blond*, *Cruel Intentions*, *The Sweetest Thing* and *Hellboy*.[190] She was born Selma Blair Beitner on June 23, 1972, in Detroit Sinai Hospital to Molly Ann and Elliot I. Beitner, both of whom were attorneys. She grew up in Southfield, attended elementary school at Hillel Day School in Farmington Hills and later graduated from Cranbrook Kingswood in Bloomfield Hills. Initially, she studied photography at Kalamazoo College before she moved at age twenty-one to New York to study at New York University. While living in the city, she also studied acting at the Stella Adler Conservatory and elsewhere.

Selma Blair in 2012. *Photo by Joella Marano. Courtesy of Wikimedia Commons.*

In 1994, Selma transferred to the University of Michigan, graduating magna cum laude with a triple major in photography, psychology and English. Afterward, she headed back to New York City to audition for roles in film and television.[191] Her breakout role came in the movie *Cruel Intentions*, which led to many other roles in both film and television. "Don't be afraid to take risks," she has said. "Some of life's greatest rewards come from stepping outside your comfort zone."[192]

For a time, she was married to Ahmet Zappa. Later, she dated fashion designer Jason Bleick, and they have one son, Arthur Saint Bleick.

In 2017, she was named a *Time* Person of the Year as one of their Silence Breakers—individuals who broke their silence surrounding sexual harassment and assault. In 2018, she was diagnosed with multiple sclerosis; she announced she was in remission as of 2021. The following year, her memoir, *Mean Baby: A Memoir of Growing Up*, was published by Alfred A. Knopf.

Pam Dawber

FARMINGTON HILLS

Pam Dawber is an actress who is perhaps best known for her role as Mindy McConnell in *Mork & Mindy*, an ABC television hit show that ran from 1978 to 1982. Her acting partner, who played Mork, was Robin Williams, who, coincidentally, also lived for many years in Oakland County. After *Mork & Mindy* came to an end, Pam Dawber played the part of Samantha Russell in *My Sister Sam* from 1986 to 1988.[193]

Robin Willams and Pam Dawber in 1978. *Courtesy of Wikimedia Commons.*

Pam was born in Detroit, the first of two daughters, to Thelma and Eugene Dawber. Her father was an advertising artist, and her mother was the owner of a stock-photography company. She graduated from North Farmington High School and later attended college at Oakland Community College. While in college, she began modeling part time and, finding success in that field, decided to forgo completing a four-year degree. Pam moved to New York City and signed with the prestigious Wilhemina Models agency. She was soon making commercials for brands such as Noxzema and Fotomat.[194]

When ABC executives viewed her screen test, they were impressed, and they enrolled her in their talent development program, from which she was paid until she received a TV role offer. It was from this program that Gary Marshall, director of *Mork & Mindy*, recruited her. Following her success with that show, Pam played the lead role of Samantha Russell in the CBS sitcom *My Sister Sam*. During this period, she married actor Mark Harmon, and they had two sons.

Although Pam acted in several films, including *Stay Tuned* with John Ritter and *I'll Remember April* with Mark Harmon, as well as in twenty-one TV movies, she remains best known for her acting in television series. In 2021, she acted in seven episodes of CBS's *NCIS*, playing the part of an investigative journalist.[195]

Christine Lahti

Birmingham

"And the Oscar goes to...Christine Lahti," a 1995 Academy Award–winning actress and director who has appeared on both Broadway and in films. Since 1979, she has acted in numerous movies, television films and theater productions. In 1989, she won a Golden Globe Award for her acting in the TV movie *No Place Like Home*. Only six years later, she received an Academy Award for her direction of and acting in the Best Live Action Short Film *Lieberman in Love*. Then, in 1998, she won both a Golden Globe and an Emmy Award for her role as Kate Austin in the CBS series *Chicago Hope*. She's also a writer and authored a book of autobiographical essays titled *True Stories from an Unreliable Eyewitness*.[196]

Christine Lahti at the Miami Film Festival Awards Night, 2016. *Photo by Alberto Tamargo. Courtesy of Wikimedia Commons.*

Christine was born in Royal Oak, Michigan, on April 4, 1950, to Elizabeth Margaret (née Tabar) and Paul Theodore Lahti but grew up in Birmingham. Her mother at various times was a nurse, a homemaker and an artist, while her father was a physician and a surgeon. She has three sisters and two brothers.

After she graduated in 1967 from Seaholm High School, Christine studied art at Florida State

University before going on to receive a bachelor's degree in drama from the University of Michigan. She also studied acting in New York City at the HB Studio. Additionally, she completed a two-year program in acting at the William Esper Studio for the Performing Arts in Manhattan. "It was not really a career choice that I had to make. It was something I knew right from the beginning. I had to be an actress…period."[197]

Christine married television director Thomas Schlamme in 1983 and has three children. She maintains homes in both Los Angeles and New York City.

Chapter 12

FARMERS AND ENVIRONMENTALISTS

SARAH VAN HOOSEN JONES (1892–1972)

ROCHESTER HILLS

Sarah Van Hoosen Jones was a major dairy and poultry farmer in Rochester Hills, but she was also a woman of many firsts. Due to her efforts, the Van Hoosen Farm, which she inherited from her grandmother and further developed for farming, was the first to produce certified milk in Michigan (meaning it was considered "safe to drink" before Grade A milk was established). It was also the first farm to fortify milk with vitamins A and D, which support healthy vision and boost calcium absorption. In the 1930s, vitamin D was also necessary to fight off rickets. Through the 1930s and '40s, the Van Hoosen Farm remained the major supplier of milk to all of Detroit.[198]

Sarah's lifelong love of farming earned her accolades along the way. She became the first woman in the United States to earn a master's degree in animal husbandry from the University of Wisconsin, as well as a PhD in animal genetics. In 1933, she was the first Michigan woman named a Master Farmer. For nine years, her farm received the award of Premier Breeder of Holstein cattle.[199]

Although Sarah Van Hoosen Jones created healthy foods for millions of people to enjoy, she herself was born weak and almost did not survive her

Sarah Van Hoosen Jones leading horses on the Van Hoosen Farm. *From the Archives of the Rochester Hills Museum at Van Hoosen Farm.*

first hours—or even her first decade—of life. Sarah was the only child of Alice Van Hoosen Jones and Joseph Comstock Jones. Close to the time of her birth, on June 23, 1892, her parents traveled from their home in Chicago to stay at the Van Hoosen Farm. Fortunately for Sarah, also staying at the farm was Dr. Bertha Van Hoosen, who was Alice's sister and a physician. Bertha helped deliver the lifeless body of baby Sarah after Alice's long, difficult labor. But Aunt Bertha was unwilling to let her niece die. For forty-five minutes, she breathed "furiously" into her tiny lungs until little Sarah finally started to breathe on her own.[200]

More unfortunate events were ahead. When Sarah was five years old, her father, Joseph, died. Once again, Aunt Bertha was there for her during that sad period. Sarah would later say it was her aunt who became like "a second father" to her. Then, at age eight, Sarah was diagnosed with diabetes insipidus, which affects how the kidneys process fluids and react to malaria. To keep Sarah alive, her mother, Alice, moved with her to the "non-malarial" climate of Santa Barbara, California, and kept young Sarah from having contact with other people. Sarah soon became a very lonely child, with only her mother, who was a former teacher, to homeschool her and keep her company.[201]

Summer was the one bright spot in Sarah's life, for that was when she and her mother would return to the Van Hoosen Farm. Once back at Stoney Creek in Oakland County, Sarah was free to roam the farm, and she grew to love the animals that lived there. Her grandmother continued to observe that Sarah was always happy and healthier physically whenever she was at the farm.

Family members described Sarah as shy, awkward and lacking in sophistication during her teenage years. Her mother wrote in her diary that Sarah "cared little for dress and cannot comb her own hair."[202] In an attempt to remedy her social awkwardness, the family took her on a tour of Europe. When they returned, Sarah entered the University of Chicago, where she graduated having studied languages. In the face of pressure from the family for her to further her education by attending medical school, as her Aunt Bertha had done, Sarah resisted and instead went on to study animal husbandry and genetics at the University of Wisconsin. After graduating, she returned to the Van Hoosen farm to practice what she had learned, and she began breeding Leghorn hens and livestock, including Holstein cattle. By that time, her grandmother Sarah was ninety-one years old and frail. However, Grandmother Sarah was so pleased to see her granddaughter happy and taking the family farm to the next level that she deeded it to her.

During the Depression, the farm branched out into retail sales and became known for its efficient, scientific and economically progressive farming methods. Sarah was finally doing the work she loved in a place she loved. She was flourishing.

Sarah always remained keenly interested in education and served on the Rochester school board from 1924 to 1961, which led to her being called the First Lady of Rochester. In addition, she was elected to two six-year terms on the State Board of Agriculture and served on the elected Board of Trustees of Michigan State University (MSU). For her contributions to agriculture and education, MSU awarded her an honorary doctorate and named Van Hoosen Hall in her honor.[202]

In 1969, Sarah had a heart attack, followed by a diagnosis of bone cancer. Her health continued to decline after that, and she died in 1972 at age eighty. She had bequeathed her farm to MSU, but the Sarah Van Hoosen Jones Questers petitioned, and MSU graciously returned the farmhouse to the Rochester Hills Community to enjoy in perpetuity. In 1994, Sarah Van Hoosen Jones was inducted into the Michigan Women's Hall of Fame.[203]

Nicole Ryan

SYLVAN LAKE

When it comes to sustainability, Nicole Ryan means business. She opened Sylvan Table, her award-winning farm-to-table restaurant, in 2021, and she has been receiving accolades ever since for using locally sourced, seasonally fresh ingredients to prepare healthy, delicious meals. Her goal is to achieve as close to a zero-waste footprint as possible, in which everything gets used and recycled in ways beneficial to our ecosystem, while she and her staff simultaneously create a warm, inviting dining experience for guests.[204]

As soon as arriving dinner guests turn off Orchard Lake Road onto Inverness Road, they can already see that Sylvan Table is the real deal. The restaurant itself is an upcycled three-hundred-year-old Maine barn that Nicole and her husband, Tim, co-owner of Ryan Construction, purchased and then had dismantled, shipped and reconstructed on the Sylvan Lake property. Thus, even the barn has received a second useful life rather than becoming landfill. They reused the barn's structural beams and older wood throughout the interior, while applying newer, sturdier stained wood to the exterior. The effect is simultaneously rustic yet current and inviting. In warmer weather, a colorful variety of flowers and other vegetation, including grapevines, grow abundantly along and between pathways, all of which are used either as food or to decorate the interior tables.

As dining guests head toward the entrance, they cannot avoid seeing an attractive complex of farm buildings, including three greenhouses where a variety of vegetables such as kale, carrots, peas and beets are grown. Plus, there are beehives that supply honey; a variety of fruit trees producing pears, apples, apricots and plums; and an outbuilding with a living roof covered in growing vegetation set atop two recycled shipping containers used for storage and as a produce-cleaning station and office.

Inside the restaurant, guests are seated according to their preference, whether that is in the solarium, complete with a fireplace that has sometimes been used for cooking but also provides a charming ambiance; at the bar

Opposite: Nicole Ryan. *Courtesy of Nicole Ryan.*

Above: Sylvan Table. *Author's collection.*

(first come, first served); or at reserved seating available on both the lower and upper levels. There is also a large outdoor dining patio.

Nicole says that all multicourse meals there are carefully thought out, taste tested and often unique, meaning that diners won't likely find similar meals elsewhere. What can be grown on the farm or with the help of Sylvan Table's local farming partners always informs the menu. Nicole thus works closely with executive chef Chris Gadulka and farm manager Rick Rigutto in the planning and execution.

Nicole is absolutely fastidious about food conservation and preparation. She insists that whenever possible, nothing be wasted or discarded. In fact, Sylvan Table is now fully certified under the PLEDGE on Food Waste, and this statement posted on the restaurant's website:

> *At Sylvan Table, we are committed to reducing food waste, practicing sustainability and joining the fight against climate change.... We are proud to announce that...we not only have reduced our food waste by 22%, but also prevented over 18,212 kg of carbon dioxide emissions by composting rather than sending our food waste into landfills.*

Information like this might make some people wonder how Nicole Ryan developed her ideas for Sylvan Table over the years. Nuggets of her personal history reveal possible influences. Nicole was born in 1965 and raised in Massachusetts. Her parents were Guidalberto Fabbri, a doctor, and Marie Irene Lagasse, an artist. Guidalberto, who was born and raised in Florence, Italy, met Marie while she was studying art in Florence. Marie, who is of French Canadian descent, came from a family that owned and operated Lagasse Amusement Company, famous in New England for its amusement parks and carnivals. In fact, Marie's father, Eli Lagasse, was the founder of the company.

After Marie completed her art studies in Florence, she and Guidalberto married and then decided to move to the United States to start their family. The couple would go on to have four children, Nicole being their youngest. Nicole grew up in Lynnfield, Massachusetts, a leafy suburb of Boston, but also has wonderful memories of spending time at the family's summer home in Gloucester. However, Nicole says that it is her mother, now in her nineties, who was extraordinarily creative and who made a lasting impression on her. "I believe I inherited my mother's artistry and her love for it," she says. "My mother belonged to a garden club and had this wonderful European flair for using plants and decorating with them." Inspired by her mother's talents, Nicole originally hoped to study art herself in college, but her father discouraged it, saying that she needed to learn a more practical skill, which ended up being accounting.

Nicole met her husband, Tim, in Oakbrook, Illinois, at Boston Chicken, the original name of Boston Market, where they both worked. Tim, who had a degree in construction management from the University of Wisconsin, built Boston Market restaurants. Nicole worked in accounting for the same company, having earned her BS in accountancy from Bentley University.

Tim and Nicole married in 1994. Their decision to settle in Michigan was based on Boston Market's moving groups of corporate employees to different parts of the country using what's called areas of dominant influence (ADI), which is information about the market and audience strength of different areas. At first, they lived in Huntington Woods; the company headquarters was in Royal Oak, an easy commute.

In the meantime, Tim and Nicole wanted to start their own construction business, and in 1995, they took the leap, incorporating Ryan Construction. Tim and Nicole then combined their complementary backgrounds in construction and accounting, and for nearly thirty years, they successfully built casual restaurants, which included Boston Market and others such as Panera, Starbucks and more.

However, Nicole had her own dream: opening a restaurant. She wanted to combine her love of cooking with fresh foods and the ideas for sustainability that her family had exposed her to while growing up. "When I was young, my family would use all parts of a roast for different purposes. Nothing was discarded," she says. "Also, there was this idea of always using what is fresh. So for fish, for example, we would go down to the docks and buy fresh fish." She also emphasizes the closeness of her family members. The way they enjoyed dinners together always stuck with her, and those memories became something she aims to emulate. "Food was and is about eating, but it's also about enjoying each other's company. I have an Italian background. That is what we do."

While in the due diligence process for the restaurant, Nicole became obsessed with learning as much as she could about cooking, cooking methods, farming, décor, sustainability and restaurant culture. She took an online course through UMass Amherst on homesteading and permaculture. In addition, she completed a culinary certificate from Schoolcraft College. "Their culinary program is incredible," she says. "They had four master chefs teaching when I was studying there, and two of them directly taught me. This is amazing because at that time, there were only sixty-five master chefs in the entire United States!"

Nicole and Tim's two adult children have also worked at Sylvan Table on and off since it opened. In 2024–25, their son, Christian Skylar, who had already earned a BS in horticulture with a concentration in sustainability, studied in Rome to complete an international master's in sustainability and circular bioeconomy. "He plans to go into business for himself. His interest is in marine farming, which includes kelp and seaweed, but he also loves to cook, like me," The Ryans' daughter, Anna, who studied journalism at Michigan State University, handles communications and related tasks for Sylvan Table. She hopes to enter the publishing world as a graphic designer for magazines and newspapers.

Nicole is proud of what she has achieved so far at Sylvan Table. "My biggest achievement is that I am finally living my dream, or at least one of them. It certainly takes a whole team, but I am finally doing what I love, and as a result, I have met all of these amazing people and have made so many other new connections. And my work family is just amazing. We are small, but I believe we are making a real difference."

Based on what she has learned and experienced over the years, Nicole offers this advice to young people who have unrealized aspirations. "Ask yourself this question: 'Why not me?' Then act on your goal. Yes, please ask yourself: 'Why not me?' And then take the leap."

IN HER OWN WORDS

Buttoning Up Tight on the Sunny Side of a Green Life

By Maura Jung

Maura Jung. *Photo by Gary Molnar. Courtesy of Maura Jung*

I am one part of a story about the building of the first certified Passive House in Michigan. This story includes my husband, Kurt Jung, and the team of others—the architect, builder and skilled tradesmen—who helped make it happen. The story took shape and evolved after a series of related occurrences and a convergence of disparate events, and it would not have happened without our having had a lifelong love of nature and a strong environmental ethic.

After deciding we wanted to live on our property, which was then a vacant former nineteenth-century farmstead in rural Rose Township (whose barn burned down in 1905 and whose house burned down in the 1950s), my husband and I began considering what type of home we wanted to build. We knew we wanted the house to be as environmentally sustainable as possible, and we set out to educate ourselves about these options.

We learned of Rose Township in northwest Oakland County when my husband accompanied our daughter, who had recently received her driver's permit, to attend a 4-H meeting in the area. This introduction to the somewhat rural, undulating topography with numerous wetlands led us to look for property of our own. We later learned that Rose Township is within the Jackson Interlobate, where glaciers made direct edge-to-edge contact, creating large amounts of glacial deposits and leading to high, hilly, rolling topography—all of which reminded me a bit of the land of my childhood in the Berkshires. We also learned that the nearby dirt Rose Center Road was once a former Native American trail, which ignited our pioneer spirit and connected us further to this beautiful area.

The beginning of discovering Passive House coincidentally began just over the border in the "other" Michigan Rose Township, which is in Ogemaw County. We were staying at an off-the-grid bed-and-breakfast near West Branch. The proprietors recommended that we subscribe to *Home Power* magazine, an indispensable resource for environmentally friendly projects of this type. It was while reading a letter to the editor by a Michigan-based woman architect in our very first issue that we first became familiar with the term *Passive House*. Within weeks, we attended a workshop where the author delivered a compelling and informative session about the Passive House. We instantly became enthusiasts. From this point, we met one of only two Michigan Passive House–trained builders at that time. They put us in touch with a former Michigan-based architecture firm, now in Maine, that designs and builds Passive Houses.

Passive House standards appealed to our science backgrounds and environmental ethic. The Passive House standard requires examining sustainable lifestyles in addition to sustainable building practices. Building a Passive House required us to think about our long-term energy consumption as well as our impact on the environment. We gravitated to the simple design and the required energy analysis at the planning stage, as well as tests throughout construction, to assure compliant performance.

A Passive House balances passive solar energy gain and storage with minimal thermal bridging. To reduce energy losses, the home is heavily insulated with an airtight building envelope and triple-

Maura Jung in front of her Passive House. *Photo by Gary Molnar. Courtesy of Maura Jung.*

glazed windows. An air exchanger/energy recovery ventilator provides continuous active ventilation, keeping rooms at a constant temperature and humidity with fresh airflow throughout. In spite of air continuously circulating, we can't feel or hear any air movement. The house is quiet and comfortable.

We used Energy Star ratings to select appliances that use the least amount of energy possible. We use a condensing dryer when the weather keeps us from hanging laundry outdoors. This kind of dryer is not vented to the outdoors in order to have one less puncture in the highly airtight building envelope. We later added solar panels, and we are close to net zero, but we are not off the grid.

The house is situated within fifteen feet of where the original farmhouse was once located. The remaining partial stone foundation from the original farmhouse became the keystone feature of a nearby stone firepit. The only intact evidence of the original barn is silo stones that are preserved in place to pay homage to the barn that once stood there.

Throughout the process of building what ended up being the first certified Passive House in Michigan, the house received a fair amount of attention. Our home won an energy efficiency award in *Fine Homebuilding* magazine and was featured in the *DTE* magazine. A diagram of our home and a close-up shot of our front door appeared in other issues of *Fine Homebuilding* magazine. We have given countless tours to interested parties, curiosity seekers, an architecture class and even to potential Passive House customers. Building our home was an interesting and exciting experience, but the story does not end there.

The land on which our Passive House sits enriched our love affair with oak barrens and the globally significant fen habitat and thus enhanced our involvement with land conservation. After settling into life in our Passive House, we began to learn more about these now rare habitats. A visit from a Michigan Department of Natural Resources biologist and a survey conducted by scientists from the Michigan State University Extension, called a Michigan Natural Features Inventory (MNFI), confirmed that our property has several acres of a high-quality fen habitat. The MNFI identified part of our property as a potential conservation area.

I began using my natural resources degree to create a land management plan, which included some hay farming, removal of invasive species, restoring parts of the property to its presettlement condition and improving the habitat for the threatened Eastern Massasauga rattlesnake. The long-term plan for our property is to continue this work and preserve it in perpetuity through a conservation easement for use by future generations.

My lifelong love of nature was evident early on and continues to this day as I steward the land on which I live and keep track of nature sightings on a daily basis. After being born on a snowy winter day in 1961 over the border in Pennsylvania, I lived my first years of life in Willingboro, New Jersey. At around the age of five, I observed, followed and eventually caught a domestic rabbit that was hopping around in the neighborhood, which we later presumed was a released Easter bunny. I cared for this rabbit for ten years. After moving to a rural part of the Berkshires in western Massachusetts and during most of my school years, I set up and ran a nature center in the basement of my family home and formed a neighborhood nature club.

When I was a junior in high school, my family moved to Michigan, where I have lived ever since. Here I received an undergraduate degree in natural resources from the University of Michigan. My graduate work in science education, curriculum and instruction and educational leadership was completed at Wayne State University. A large part of my career was spent working in environmental and science education in a variety of settings, including nature centers, a natural history museum and schools. A lifelong love of nature and a strong environmental ethic begins and ends the story of the first certified Passive House in Michigan.

NOTES

Chapter 1

1. Smith, *Biographical Record*, 243.
2. Ibid., 244.
3. Pielack, *Saginaw Trail*, 64.
4. Smith, *Biographical Record*, 245.
5. Seeley, *History of Oakland County*, 259.
6. Youth for Understanding.
7. Ibid.
8. To view the extent of the devastation, see War Stories, "The Impossible Cleanup That Followed the End of WW2," YouTube, November 15, 2024, https://youtu.be/XoA3YzkmyQ8.
9. Youth for Understanding.
10. Youth for Understanding.
11. Rachel Josephine Andresen papers, 1948–1986, Background, University of Michigan (UM), Bentley Historical Library, Ann Arbor, Michigan.
12. Ibid.
13. Ibid.
14. Ibid.
15. Ibid.
16. Ibid.
17. Ibid.
18. Youth for Understanding.

19. Ibid.
20. Rachel Josephine Andresen papers.
21. Michigan Women Forward, "Rachel Andresen."
22. Rachel Josephine Andresen papers.

Chapter 2

23. Avery, *Historic Michigan*, 194.
24. Ibid.
25. Lathrup, *Gateways to Happiness*, 14.
26. U.S. Bureau of Labor Statistics, "Women in the Labor Force: A Databook," 2022. https://www.bls.gov.
27. Lathrup Village Historical Society, "About Louise: Louise Lathrup Kelley," March 6, 2016, https://lathrupvillagehistoricalsociety.wordpress.com.
28. Recollections of Louise Lathrup Driscoll, daughter's notes, n.d.
29. Lathrup, *Gateways to Happiness*, 16a.
30. Lathrope Family Genealogy, "Origin of the Name," https://lathro.pe.
31. Louise Lathrup, "Louise Lathrup's California Bungalow Subdivision," Cost Sheet No. 1, C.E. Reichle Co., March 20, 1925.
32. Lathrup Village Historical Society, "On This Day in Lathrup Village History," June 6, 2022, https://lathrupvillagehistoricalsociety.wordpress.com.
33. Lathrup Village Historical Society, "The Inglorious End of Town Hall," May 17, 2021, https://lathrupvillagehistoricalsociety.wordpress.com.
34. Hagman, "Lathrup Village," 208.
35. National Park Service, "National Register Information System," November 2, 2013, https://npgallery.nps.gov/NRHP.
36. City of Lathrup Village, "Community Groups," http://www.lathrupvillage.org.
37. Jamie L. LaReau, "GM CEO Barra Says Trump Administration and Automaker Share Many Goals," *Detroit Free Press*, December 11, 2024.
38. Michelle Thompson, "GM to Offer Bidirectional Vehicle-to-Home Charging for Coming Models," August 9, 2023, Repairer Driven News, https://www.repairerdrivennews.com.
39. Jamie L. LaReau, "GM CEO Mary Barra's Rare, Behind-the-Scenes Interview: Who She Relies On in 'Lonely Job,'" *Detroit Free Press*, January 26, 2023.

40. Ibid.
41. Ibid.
42. Colby, *Road to Power*, 12.
43. Ibid., 43.
44. Ibid., 50.
45. *Star Wars Episode IV: A New Hope* (1977), 1:55:54.
46. Mary Liz Curtin, interview by Christine Blackwell, May 8, 2024, at Leon & Lulu.

Chapter 3

47. Jewish Women's Archive, "Hilda R. Gage," https://jwa.org.
48. Ibid.
49. Ann Zaniewski, "Longtime Oakland County Judge Hilda Gage Dies at Age 71," *Oakland Press*, June 17, 2021.
50. Ibid.
51. Tom Kirvan, "Gold Standard: State Appeals Court Judge Served as Inspiration to All," Legal News, September 10, 2010, https://legalnews.com.
52. Ibid.
53. Ibid.
54. Zaniewski, "Longtime Oakland County Judge."
55. Kirvan, "Gold Standard."
56. Jewish Women's Archive, "Gage."
57. Kirvan, "Gold Standard."

Chapter 4

58. Deborah J. Remer, *Soldiers, Scholars and Pioneers: A Tour of the Stoney Creek Cemetery* (Rochester Hills Museum at Van Hoosen Farm, 2005), 12.
59. Thalmann, *Women at Van Hoosen Farm*, 6.
60. Ibid., 7.
61. Ibid., 7.
62. American Association for State and Local History (AASLA), "Explore the Home of Dr. Bertha Van Hoosen, Founder of the American Women's Medical Association at AASLH/MMA 2016," https://aaslh.org.
63. Ibid.
64. Thalmann, *Women at Van Hoosen Farm*, 4.

65. AASLA, "Explore the Home."
66. Remer, *Soldiers, Scholars and Pioneers*, 12.
67. Thalmann, *Women at Van Hoosen Farm*, 7.
68. Ibid.
69. Ibid.
70. Dr. Petra Huck, interview by Christine Blackwell, June 7, 2024, at Cranbrook Institute of Science.

Chapter 5

71. Lindbergh, *War Within and Without*, 305–06.
72. PBS, "Anne Morrow Lindbergh," American Experience, https://www.pbs.org.
73. Ibid.
74. Edwards, "Anne Morrow Lindbergh."
75. Ibid.
76. Lindbergh, *War Within and Without*, 279.
77. Ibid., 281–82.
78. Ibid., 313.
79. Ibid., 318–19.
80. Ibid., 377.
81. Edwards, "Anne Morrow Lindbergh."
82. Christian, *Su Arte, Su Vida*, 20.
83. "Nora Chapa Mendoza Named 2024 Kresge Eminent Artist," *El Central Hispanic News*, January 25, 2024.
84. Nora Chapa Mendoza, interview by Christine Blackwell, September 24, 2024, West Bloomfield. In particular, Nora treasures the letter to her from Cesar Chavez. Nora's daughter, Laurie, is also an artist.
85. Ibid.
86. Ibid. *Fire Ants* is a mixed-media piece. In addition to the large ants hanging from one edge are smaller ants, painted to show them crawling all around the toddler.
87. Mohr, *My Life Through Paintings*, 10.
88. Ibid. Laurie wept as she watched her mother read the words through the painting's keyhole.
89. Christian, *Su Arte, Su Vida*, 29.
90. Ibid.
91. Ibid.

92. Ibid.
93. Ibid., 44.
94. Christian, "Trailblazing Chicana Painter."
95. Christian, *Su Arte, Su Vida*, 34.
96. Bilek, *Great Female Artists of Detroit*, 71.
97. Christian, *Su Arte, Su Vida*, 26.
98. Mendoza interview.

Chapter 6

99. Ruff, "Annemarie Bondy Roeper," 3.
100. Ibid.
101. Ibid.
102. Ruth Seymour, "She Was Part of LIT from the Start," *Detroit Free Press*, December 28, 1982.
103. Ibid.
104. Dick Frederick, quoted in Seymour, "She Was Part of LIT."
105. Seymour, "She Was Part of LIT."
106. From a telephone conversation with Bruce Annett Jr., university historian, Lawrence Technological University (LTU), summer of 2024, which included his reference to "Back to School with the Henry Ford Trade School," Henry Ford Archives, Digital Collections, September 21, 2021, https://www.thehenryford.org.
107. Contribution from Bruce Annett Jr., university historian, LTU, summer 2024.
108. Ibid.
109. Author's conversation with Genevieve Dooley, circa 1976.
110. Ibid.
111. Recollections from the author about Genevieve Dooley and the reason for this book's dedication made in her memory.

Chapter 7

112. Rosemary Hakim Bannon, interview by Christine Blackwell, with Contessa Bannon contributing, June 25, 2024, Bloomfield Township Public Library.
113. Ibid.

114. See Journalism Hall of Fame, Past Inductees, "Charlotte 'Tavy' Stone: Fashion Writer, *The Detroit News*," https://mijournalismhalloffame.org.
115. Bannon interview.
116. Recollections of Norm and Christine Blackwell, who lived on Stratford Lane during the 1970s and whose mother, Mrs. Edward Blackwell, was employed by builder Paul Johnson as the Cranbrook Manor property manager and, with Edward, purchased one of the townhouses.
117. Ibid.
118. Lynch & Sons Funeral Directors, "Pamela Eldred-Robbins," July 12, 2022, https://www.lynchandsonsclawson.com.
119. Ibid.
120. Ibid.
121. Ibid.
122. NJ Advance Media, "Miss America 1970, Pamela Eldred-Robbins, Dead at 74," https://www.njadvancemedia.com.

Chapter 8

123. Terry Pochert, "Bell-Hansen, Rita (nee Connolly)," Broadcasting Vault, June 28, 2023, https://broadcastingvault.com.
124. Gregory A. Fournier, "Rita Bell's Prize Movie," Fornology.com, March 2, 2023, https://fornology.blogspot.com.
125. Ibid.
126. Ibid.
127. Pochert, "Bell-Hansen, Rita."
128. Fournier, "Rita Bell's Prize Movie."
129. Myesha Johnson, "Doris Biscoe, Trailblazing Newswoman at WXYZ, Dies at Age 77," *Detroit News*, June 9, 2024.
130. Bruce Haring, "Doris Biscoe Dies: Veteran Detroit TV Reporter and News Anchor Was 77," Deadline, June 9, 2024.
131. Ibid.
132. Johnson, "Doris Biscoe."
133. Sande Drew, telephone interview by Christine Blackwell, July 7, 2024.
134. Ibid.
135. Ibid.

Chapter 9

136. Baldwin Public Library, "History," https://www.baldwinlib.org.
137. Painter, *Baldwin Library at 75*, 6–7.
138. Ibid.
139. Pastor, *Woman's Work*, 17. See also McMechan, *Book of Birmingham*, 105.
140. Baldwin Public Library, "History."
141. Meadow Brook, "History," https://meadowbrookhall.org.
142. Pitrone and Elwart, *John Dodge Story*, 8.
143. Ibid., 18.
144. Ibid., 22.
145. Ibid., 23.
146. Ibid., 26.
147. Madelyn Rzadkowolski, "The Place to See and Be Seen," *Meadow Brook Magazine*, 90th Anniversary Issue, Spring 2019, 18–19.
148. Pitrone and Elwart, *John Dodge Story*, 27.
149. Ibid., 27–28.
150. Meadow Brook, https://meadowbrookhall.org.
151. Michigan State University College of Veterinary Medicine, "Matilda Wilson and the Meadow Brook Farm," https://cvm.msu.edu.
152. Wilson, *Place in the Country*, x.
153. Ibid.
154. Nancy Hague, interview by Christine Blackwell, April 26, 2024, Autumn House, Bloomfield Hills.
155. Dr. Indra Saini, interview by Christine Blackwell, October 24, 2024, Troy.
156. Beverly Johnson Wiggins, interview by Christine Blackwell, April 11, 2024, Bloomfield Township Public Library.
157. Mia Materka, interview by Christine Blackwell, April 17, 2024, Bloomfield Hills.
158. Fox and Cameron, *Farmington Childhood: The Watercolors of Lillian Drake Avery.*

Chapter 10

159. Brittanica, "Aretha Franklin," https://www.britannica.com.
160. Maggie Maloney, "Aretha Franklin's Most Iconic Quotes of All Time," *Town & Country*, August 16, 2018, https://www.townandcountrymag.com.
161. Ibid.
162. Brittanica, "Aretha Franklin."

163. Michael Hill, "Inductees and Nominees," Rock & Roll Hall of Fame, https://rockhall.com.
164. Ibid.
165. Ibid.
166. "Aretha Franklin," Biography, September 15, 2021, https://www.biography.com.
167. Ibid.
168. Ibid.
169. Maloney, "Aretha Franklin's Most Iconic Quotes."
170. Emy LaCroix, "Aretha Franklin's 4 Children: All About Clarence, Edward, Teddy and Kecalf," *People*, March 28, 2024, https://people.com.
171. University of Detroit Mercy Libraries, "Aretha Franklin: Honorary Doctor of Music," https://libraries.udmercy.edu.
172. Solomon, *Queen Next Door*, 119.
173. Maloney, "Aretha Franklin's Most Iconic Quotes."
174. Acting Magazine, "What Percentage of Actors Make It Big?" https://actingmagazine.com.
175. Martha Ross, "Review: Madonna Does 'My Best' in Spectacular, Frustrating SF Show," *Mercury News*, February 29, 2024, https://www.mercurynews.com.
176. Gabriel, "Take a Bow."
177. Campbell, *Complete Fan Guide*, 14.
178. Ibid., 14–15.
179. Gabriel, *Madonna*, 40–41, 406.
180. Campbell, *Complete Fan Guide*, 19.
181. Graham, "Madonna Shows Vulnerability."
182. Ibid.

Chapter 11

183. IMDb, "Patricia Ellis: Biography," https://www.imdb.com.
184. Cladrite Radio, "10 Things You Should Know About Patricia Ellis," YouTube, May 20, 2022.
185. Bill Chappell, "Actress and Singer Elaine Stritch Has Died," NPR, July 17, 2014, https://www.npr.org.
186. Rex Reed, "Small-Time Woody, Expert Tracey," *New York Observer*, May 22, 2000.

187. Robert Viagas, "Theatre Hall of Fame 1996," *Playbill*, January 30, 1996.
188. Maddie McGay, "These States Produce the Most Celebs," Yahoo, October 20, 2023, https://www.yahoo.com.
189. IMDb, "Kristen Bell: Biography," https://www.imdb.com.
190. *People*, "Selma Blair," https://www.people.com.
191. Blair, *Mean Baby*, 131.
192. Bookey Book Summary, "30 Best Selma Blair Quotes with Image," https://www.bookey.app.
193. Biography, "Pam Dawber," https://www.biography.com.
194. Marshall and Marshall, *Wake Me When It's Funny*, 16.
195. Naledi Ushe, "Mark Harmon's Wife Pam Dawber to Join Him on 'NCIS' for 4 Episodes," *People*, March 17, 2021.
196. IMDb, "Christine Lahti: Biography," https://www.imdb.com.
197. Enquoted, "Top 24 Quotes by Christine Lahti," https://www.enquoted.com.

Chapter 12

198. Thalmann, *Women at Van Hoosen Farm*, 9.
199. Tiffany Dziurman, "Rochester's Most Famous Women Include Dairy Farmer, Minister and One Who Formed OU," Patch, March 2011, https://patch.com.
200. Thalmann, *Women at Van Hoosen Farm*, 5.
201. Ibid., 8.
202. Ibid.
203. Ibid., 10.
204. Nicole Ryan, interview by Christine Blackwell, August 10, 2024.

SELECTED BIBLIOGRAPHY

Avery, Lillian Drake, ed. *Historic Michigan: Land of the Great Lakes.* Vol. 3. National Historical Association, 1924.

Bilek, Suzanne. *Great Female Artists of Detroit.* The History Press, 2012.

Blair, Selma. *Mean Baby: A Memoir of Growing Up.* Alfred A. Knopf, 2022.

Campbell, Kathy, ed. *A Complete Fan Guide to Madonna.* U.S. News/A360 Media, 2024.

Christian, Nichole, ed. *Su Arte, Su Vida: Nora Chapa Mendoza.* Kresge Foundation, 2024.

Christian, Nichole. "Trailblazing Chicana Painter Nora Chapa Mendoza Named 2024 Kresge Eminent Artist; Annual Award Now $100K." Kresge Foundation, August 12, 2024.

Colby, Laura. *Road to Power.* John Wiley & Sons, 2015.

College for Creative Studies. "Nora Chapa Mendoza Named Kresge Eminent Artist for 2024." January 25, 2024. https://www.ccsdetroit.edu.

Curtin, Mary Liz. *A Shopkeeper's Manual.* Wicked Queen Press, 2006.

Edwards, Leslie. "Anne Morrow Lindbergh: The Cranbrook Connection." *Cranbrook Kitchen Sink* (blog), Cranbrook Center for Collections and Research, March 20, 2015. https://cranbrookkitchensink.com.

Fox, Jean M., and John B. Cameron. *A Farmington Childhood: The Watercolors of Lillian Drake Avery.* Farmington Hills Historical Commission, 1985.

Frye, Barbara. "Society Ladies and the Daughters of the American Revolution." *Oakland Gazette* 57, no. 1 (March 2024).

Gabriel, Mary. *Madonna: A Rebel Life.* Little, Brown, 2023.

———. "Take a Bow, Madonna." *New York Times*, August 15, 2023.

Graham, Adam. "Madonna Shows Vulnerability at Homecoming Concert: 'I Hope You're Proud of Me, Detroit!'" *Detroit News*, January 16, 2024.

Hagman, Arthur A., ed. *Oakland County Book of History: Oakland County, Michigan Sesqui-Centennial 1820–1970*. Oakland County Sesquicentennial Committee, 1970.

Harris, Fran. *Focus: Michigan Women 1701–1977*. Michigan Coordinating Committee of the National Commission on the Observance of Women's Year, n.d.

Hyde, Michael. *The Dodge Brothers: Detroit's Automotive Geniuses*. Meadow Brook Press, 2014.

Jones, Sara Van Hoosen. *Chronicle of Van Hoosen Centenary Farm*. Rochester Hills Museum at Van Hoosen Farm, 1969.

Lathrup Village Historical Society. "About Louise." October 6, 2016. https://lathrupvillagehistoricalsociety.wordpress.com.

Lathrup, Louise. *Gateways to Happiness: A Book of House Plans and a Home-Planning Service*. 2nd ed. Speaker-Hines Printing, 1924.

Lindbergh, Anne Morrow. *The Steep Ascent*. Harcourt Brace, 1944.

———. *War Within and Without*. Harcourt Brace Jovanovich, 1980.

Lindbergh, Charles A. *The Wartime Journals of Charles A. Lindbergh*. Harcourt Brace Jovanovich, 1970.

Marshall, Garry, and Lori Marshall. *Wake Me When It's Funny: How to Break into Show Business and Stay There*. Newmarket Press, 1995.

McMechan, Jervis Bell. *The Book of Birmingham*. Birmingham Historical Board, 1976.

Meadow Brook. https://meadowbrookhall.org.

Michigan Women Forward. "Rachel Andresen." https://miwf.org.

Mohr, Matthew M. *My Life Through Paintings: Selected Works from Nora Chapa Mendoza*. Books by Violins, March 28, 2012.

Painter, Patricia Scollard. *Baldwin Public Library at 75*. Baldwin Public Library, 1975.

Pastor, Joni Faye. *Woman's Work: The Story of Martha Baldwin*. Baldwin Public Library, 1976.

Pielack, Leslie K. *The Saginaw Trail: From Native American Path to Woodward Avenue*. The History Press, 2018.

Pitrone, Jean Maddern, and Joan Potter Elwart. *The John Dodge Story*. Meadow Brook Hall Publication, Oakland University, n.d.

Psarianos, Laurie, with Nora Chapa Mendoza. "Nora Chapa Mendoza." *Aztlan: A Journal of Chicano Studies* 49, no. 1 (Spring 2014): 227–41.

Ruff, Marcia (Roeper School Historian). "Annmarie Bondy Roeper" and "The Roeper School." Roeper School, February 2017.

Smith, Edward C. *Biographical Record: Biographical Sketches of Leading Citizens of Oakland County, Michigan.* Biographical Publishing, 1903.

Solomon, Linda. *The Queen Next Door: Aretha Franklin, An Intimate Portrait.* Wayne State University Press, 2019.

Thalmann, Maureen. *Museum Visitor Collector's Edition: The Women at Van Hoosen Farm.* Rochester Hills Museum at Van Hoosen Farm, 2010.

Troester, Rosalie Riegle, ed. *Historic Women of Michigan: A Sesquicentennial Celebration.* Michigan Women's Studies Association, 1987.

Van Hoosen, Bertha. *Petticoat Surgeon.* Rochester Hills Museum at Van Hoosen Farm, 1947. Reprinted 1994.

Welch, David. *Charging Ahead: Mary Barra and the Reinvention of an American Icon.* HarperCollins Leadership, 2022.

Wilson, Matilda Rausch Dodge. *A Place in the Country: Matilda Wilson's Personal Guidebook to Meadow Brook Hall.* Oakland University, 1998.

Youth for Understanding. https://yfu.org.

INDEX

F

G

H

J

K

L

M

N

O

P

R

S

T

V

W

Y

Z

ABOUT THE AUTHOR

Christine Blackwell is a former editorial director for Harcourt Brace and Houghton Mifflin Harcourt. She now enjoys researching and writing about the people and places of Metro Detroit, where she grew up. She is a member of several historical societies, including the Oakland County Pioneer and Historical Society and the Bloomfield Historical Society. Over the years, she has also taught English part time at Lawrence Technological University, Michigan State University and Valencia College (Florida). She holds degrees in humanities (English and architecture concentrations), journalism and creative writing from Lawrence Technological University, Michigan State University and the University of Glasgow, respectively. Her hobbies include recurve archery and art. This is her second book, the first being *Bloomfield Hills: Home of Cranbrook*, also published by The History Press.